DIFFICULT TEXTS

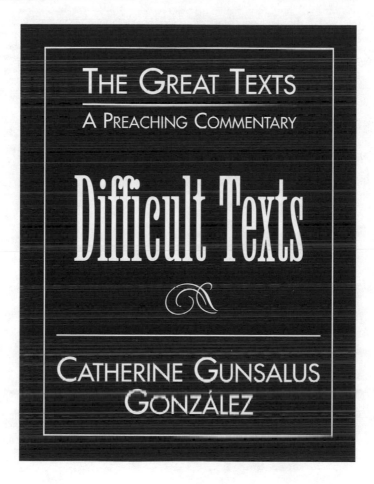

THE GREAT TEXTS

A PREACHING COMMENTARY

Difficult Texts

CATHERINE GUNSALUS
GONZÁLEZ

Abingdon Press
Nashville

THE GREAT TEXTS: A PREACHING COMMENTARY
DIFFICULT TEXTS

Copyright © 2005 by Abingdon Press

All rights reserved.

This book is printed on acid-free paper.

Library of Congress Cataloging-in-Publication Data

González, Catherine Gunsalus.
  Difficult texts : a preaching commentary / Catherine Gunsalus González.
     p. cm.—(The great texts)
  Includes bibliographical references and index.
  ISBN 0-687-05511-3 (binding: pbk. : alk. paper)

  1. Bible—Criticism, interpretation, etc.   2. Preaching.   I. Title.   II. Series.
  BS511.3.G665 2005
  251—dc22

                                                                          2004021616

05 06 07 08 09 10 11 12 13 14—10 9 8 7 6 5 4 3 2 1

MANUFACTURED IN THE UNITED STATES OF AMERICA

To Justo—

with whom even the difficult
is an adventure of faith

Contents

Introduction

What makes a biblical text difficult? Whenever and wherever Christians read the Bible, two things can be said with confidence. First, because all human beings, and therefore all human societies, are sinful, some of the demands or expectations set forth in Scripture will be difficult for people to accept. Second, because all human beings and all human societies are unique, the difficulties will not be the same. What one person may find easy and even comforting to hear in God's word, another will find exceedingly challenging. That is to say, although Christians in every setting will find the gospel challenging, the challenges are not the same. All people have those things for which they must repent, but sins are infinitely variable. Therefore, when we speak of difficult or challenging passages of Scripture, the difficulty is intrinsic not necessarily to the passage itself, but to the way in which it confronts us in our own particular situation.

There are occasions when specific issues become a dominant subject of controversy in the church and probably also in the wider society, and biblical passages that directly touch the topic become themselves the focus of debate. This was true in the nineteenth century on the issue of slavery. In more recent history, anti-Semitism, the ordination of women, homosexuality, and capital punishment all have become the subject of heated controversy. At such times, the church must struggle with particular texts that are indeed difficult for it. Often these texts are the assumed foundation for the earlier common opinion on the issue. Opinion has become divided, and so now the interpretation of those particular passages is the subject of great debate. Many articles and books have been written on such passages, and there is no need here to rehearse the arguments on these topics again.

There are other passages, however, that have not been the subject of such specific controversy; and yet were we to preach on them we and the congregation would immediately classify them as difficult texts indeed. It is some of these texts that we will consider in this study.

The church in every period of its history, and in the midst of every cultural setting, has found and will continue to find the gospel challenging. At least some within the church will discover challenges. Others will avoid or soften the hard edges of the gospel and find little that will cause them to alter their lives. Most of us probably find we respond in both ways, seeing some clear challenges, but also softening them so that they will not be so demanding. But we are left with a sense of guilt, however hidden, that somehow we are not living as faithfully as we should.

At the same time, though we may say without doubt that all human societies are sinful, we cannot say that all aspects of any society are contrary to the gospel. Surely in every culture there are elements that are parallel to the life God intends us to live. Sin has not totally destroyed God's good creation, however much it has warped it. What God created us to be and what the gospel calls us to be are not two different things. Because sin has damaged God's good creation, redemption needs to put us back on the right track. But some aspects of God's original intention have remained in all societies, though not always the same aspects. It is difficult for us who are immersed from birth in our own culture to be very clear about what particular parts of our society's assumptions are indeed parallel to or influenced by the gospel, and what parts are quite contrary to it. This is especially true in societies where the church historically has been very much a part of the culture. It is usually easier for a Christian from a different culture to see conflicts between our cultural assumptions and the gospel we proclaim. That is probably why we often resent the "outsiders" and say they simply do not understand our situation.

The task of sorting out what is and what is not good about the way we are living is really the work of prophets among God's people. And yet, not all who claim to be prophets are that. This was the problem in ancient Israel. Isaiah complained that the people "say to the seers, 'Do not see'; and to the prophets, 'Do not prophesy to us what is right; speak to us smooth things, prophesy illusions'" (Isaiah 30:10). A century and a half later, Jeremiah had the same complaint about Judah:

> Then I said: "Ah, Lord GOD! Here are the prophets saying to them, 'You shall not see the sword, nor shall you have famine, but I will give you true peace in this place.'" And the LORD said to me: The prophets are prophesying lies in my name; I did not send them, nor did I command them or speak to them. They are prophesying to you a lying vision, worthless divination, and the deceit of their own minds. (Jeremiah 14:13-14)

The rejection of the "outsider" functioned in ancient Israel as well as now. Remember Amos, the prophet from the Southern Kingdom of Judah sent to prophesy in the Northern Kingdom of Israel, in its royal city of Bethel. Both peoples worshiped the God of Israel. The Northern Kingdom, however, had become wealthy and self-satisfied, filled with injustice. Amos spoke harshly against these things, prophesying that God was about to destroy the Northern Kingdom because of its sinful ways, its disobedience to God. Then, we are told,

> Amaziah, the priest of Bethel, sent to King Jeroboam of Israel, saying, "Amos has conspired against you in the very center of the house of Israel; the land is not able to bear all his words. For thus Amos has said, 'Jeroboam shall die by the sword, and Israel must go into exile away from his land.'" And Amaziah said to Amos, "O seer, go, flee away to the land of Judah, earn your bread there, and prophesy there; but never again prophesy at Bethel, for it is the king's sanctuary, and it is a temple of the kingdom." (Amos 7:10-13)

The prophets as well as the nation may find it easier to believe that God agrees with their way of life, especially if they have a long history of assuming they are indeed God's people, than to accept the fact that God is really in radical disagreement with some aspects of their society. It is also easier to assume that whatever in the society makes them uncomfortable are things God detests than to believe that some of the elements of the culture they most enjoy are in fact far from the gospel of God. This may not even be a conscious falsifying of God's word, but simply the unconscious assumption that God could not possibly be opposed to that which God's people in that society hold as basic truth. It takes a great immersion in God's word, and the faithfulness that truly seeks God's will, to overcome our inherent tendency to assume that what we are comfortable with and what God wants are the same thing. It takes an ability to transcend our own culture, an ability that is not easily acquired.

A high price may be demanded from those who do hear in God's word something that truly challenges a basic assumption of their own society. Theirs will not be a welcome word. Those who speak it may be scorned as foolish, irrelevant, or disloyal to the nation or group. They may be accused of abandoning their heritage and even of being "unchristian" because their beliefs go against what others, even those in the church, understand.

THE TASK OF THIS STUDY

What we will be concerned about in this study is not so much the variations in individual Christians, significant as those may be. There will always be those in the same congregation who are of different personality types, or in very different personal circumstances. Some will be in grief, while others are rejoicing. The preacher, of course, needs to be aware of these things; but this is not the theme of our study. Rather, we will be concerned with the significance of the cultural settings and social conditions under which groups of Christians live out their lives and their hearing the biblical word. Within a single congregation, these basic social and cultural conditions are much more likely to be common to all. If the nation is at war, all will probably feel they have the same enemy. The same general assumptions about family duties will be present in a given society or subculture.

When we look at the challenges of the gospel and the difficulty of preaching such challenges, we must clarify why a *particular* demand is contrary to characteristics of a *particular* society. The demands are quite specific, not general issues that all Christians in all situations would find equally difficult or disturbing. The character of the gospel is always the same, and the kind of life to which it calls us is the same. But because of the different settings, some of these gospel imperatives will find ready acceptance in some places, and yet be seen as almost impossible in others.

SOME EXAMPLES

Let us look briefly at several passages to illustrate this basic assumption. We will look at passages dealing with three different issues.

The first issue is words about family ties. Remember the word of Jesus as recorded in Luke 14:26-27: "Whoever comes to me and does not hate father and mother, wife and children, brothers and sisters, yes, and even life itself, cannot be my disciple. Whoever does not carry the cross and follow me cannot be my disciple." Most of us would probably find these words a little unsettling. For some Christians in our own society, especially those who are steeped in the extreme individualism of our culture, it is readily imaginable that discipleship could demand forsaking family ties. In fact, some recent interpretations lean toward seeing the gospel as a form of self-fulfillment or self-development or achieving our own human potential that can override all other duties. People who hold to this individualism would see their duty as first to themselves and not to others. In fact, in some groups there might be little to distinguish duty to self and duty to God. These words about cutting family ties might well be used as a justification for a present lifestyle that has its roots in wider cultural patterns and not in the gospel; that is, in the cult of individualism. Such a mentality, however, would find the rest of the passage, the words about carrying the cross, much more demanding.

However, imagine Christians in an Asian setting that is steeped in the duties of family, such as a traditional Confucian culture. They might have a difficult time with Jesus' words about hating father and mother. The Confucian culture is much older than the church in such a society. There are many first-generation Christians, many of whom have been rejected by their families because they have joined the church. The duty of children to their parents is overwhelmingly strong in a Confucian society. Individualism is not part of the tradition. How then can these words be understood? For a new Christian who has decided to be part of the church, such words might bring a strange comfort that

God well understands the choice that had to be made between family and faithfulness. The text would not be the justification of a life based upon the assumptions of the wider society, but a choice based on the gospel itself. For Christians in that society, these words might represent the continuing challenge of the gospel over against the basic attitudes of the culture. The words might be softened or ignored, but they would clearly challenge some very basic assumptions in a way that they do not in a Western industrial setting. At the same time, in such a culture the words about denying oneself might take on cultural connotations not meant by the gospel; and those would have to be sorted out. Therefore in this brief passage the first half might present less of a problem in Western society than would the second half. In a congregation in an Eastern society, the problems could be reversed.

Many first-generation Christians, those in places where the church is fairly recent, would find their own lives showing the truth of the words of Jesus in Luke 12:51-53:

> Do you think that I have come to bring peace to the earth? No, I tell you, but rather division! From now on five in one household will be divided, three against two and two against three; they will be divided: father against son and son against father, mother against daughter and daughter against mother, mother-in-law against her daughter-in-law and daughter-in-law against mother-in-law.

At the same time, many in our own culture, where the church is not a recent creation, will assume that the church is what can hold families together and make for peace in the household. Obviously, the social setting makes all the difference in the world.

In a similar vein, the words in Luke 18:29-30 would be good news to those who have had to sacrifice family ties in order to be faithful: "Truly I tell you, there is no one who has left house or wife or brothers or parents or children, for the sake of the kingdom of God, who will not get back very much more in this age, and in the age to come eternal life." Those from a Western culture who break their family ties out of a non-Christian individualism would hardly find positive the thought that they were going to receive even more family members than they gave up. But for first-generation Christians, the congregation often becomes exactly that: a new family, with all of the obligations and joys that families entail. Although because they have become Christians they may have lost the family into which they were born, in this new family they are related to others by faith rather than by blood.

There may seem to be a great difference between our Western setting and that of a first-generation Christian in some Asian congregation. But as our society becomes increasingly secular we are finding more "first-generation" Christians in our own churches. That is to say, there are some young adults whose grandparents might have been part of churches, but whose own parents have had no contact with any church since long before their children were born. Perhaps even the grandparents left any active participation before their own children were born. Now these young people are attracted to the church, and they may find themselves scorned by family members as well as friends and colleagues. It is a different kind of first-generation setting, but there may be some parallels. Texts that were not difficult in our churches may become so, and comforting ones that have not had a place in our religious lives may take on new meaning because of changes in our own culture.

The second issue is enemies. In Matthew 5:44 we are told to love our enemies and pray for those who persecute us. If we live in relative peace, we are likely to interpret "enemies" to be those people whom we personally find unpleasant. They may be difficult family members or coworkers or neighbors. We see this command as calling us to love them and pray for them. That is good and is to be encouraged. However, if we are to realize the full meaning of this passage, we cannot overlook the term "persecution." Most of what we suffer at the hands of very difficult people in our lives is not persecution. Let us imagine ourselves in a situation of open conflict, of clear oppression, of outright persecution, based on group identity and not on personal interaction. For instance, think of the former Yugoslavia, where one ethnic group has been pitted against another, where hostilities going back centuries continue to erupt. Or think of the situation in the Middle East in which Israelis and Palestinians claim the same land, the same houses. Think of ancient hatred played out in Northern Ireland, in South Africa, in racial tensions in the United States. If this is what is meant by "enemies," how much more difficult it is to fulfill the commandment. It can often appear treasonous to our own group, especially if we called on our friends and neighbors to love our common enemy. For those of us who generally think of "enemies" as only those individuals we find hard to like, how helpful it would be to speak with people who understand how very difficult the command really is. In our relatively comfortable settings we might find the command easy. If we imagined ourselves in one of these other settings, it might look much harder.

The events of September 11 did give us some awareness of this wider meaning of enemies and the difficulty of loving them. In many communities across the United States, in the wake of the attacks, churches reached out to local Muslims, trying to be clear that "the enemy" was not Islam or all Arabs. At the same time, any word about forgiveness for those who were responsible for the attacks seemed close to impossible. Perhaps congregations are ready to understand the full import of these biblical words now in a way they could not earlier.

Where the enemy is the enemy of the whole people and not simply a personal, individual antagonist, a process of demonization often takes place. The enemy is viewed as subhuman, as not worthy of normal human considerations. We see this in time of war when caricatures show all members of the enemy group as evil. Political cartoons and posters about patriotism demonstrate this tendency. Language often changes so that derogatory names for the enemy become standard and acceptable. All of this is part of the human tendency to justify treating the enemy in ways that would otherwise be unacceptable. Because of this process of demonization children are brought up to assume that the enemy is not worthy of love or forgiveness. The whole society is in general agreement on this issue. For that reason the enemy of the group is much harder to love than simply one's own personal enemy. In the case of a personal enemy, there are others around us who do not view that person in the same way. Our personal attitude toward someone does not have the force of the whole society behind it.

To love enemies when the rest of the group is demonizing them is a very difficult task. It carries risk. The early Christians could have demonized all the officials of the Roman Empire. Instead, they made it a normative practice to pray for the emperor and the empire, even at times when there was persecution by the empire against the church. Christians must be on constant vigilance against this process of demonization in the wider society. They must be able to recognize when it has happened—even when it is barely beginning—and speak out against it. In the former Yugoslavia, and in Northern Ireland—here we can recognize the problem of stereotyping the enemy. Often we wonder why the people there cannot simply learn to live together. They are not our enemies, and so the problem seems relatively simple. It is much more difficult for us to recognize the same process in our own society, whether it concerns racial groups, the poor, or political enemies of the nation. As long as we view this passage as dealing mainly with our own private enemies, we will not tackle the much more difficult task.

A third example issue is economic security. In Luke 18:18-23, we find the account of the rich young ruler who came to Jesus. After ascertaining that the young man had obeyed the commandments all of his life, Jesus told him that what the young man lacked was to sell all of his possessions and follow Jesus. The man turned away. In verse 24, Jesus comments, "How hard it is for those who have wealth to enter the kingdom of God!" Obviously such words would be much more challenging to a person who has wealth than to one who does not. In fact, a person in a low-economic status might well find these words no challenge at all, but positively comforting. They might even be used to give the person comforted a sense of spiritual superiority over those who are richer, though pride in one's spiritual superiority is not a Christian virtue.

The person who has wealth, however, will probably see in these words a clear challenge. The wealthy person may seek to interpret that it is the love of money that was the problem here, and not wealth itself. The person may take comfort in the fact that others are much wealthier and still are considered good Christians. But the passage will remain haunting, and its challenge will not easily go away.

In a similar manner, in Matthew 6:25, Jesus says, "Do not worry about your life what you will eat or what you will drink, or about your body, what you will wear." The person who is economically secure may find these words fairly easy to abide by. His or her immediate needs are taken care of. The person's concerns for long-term economic security are assumed to lie beyond the import of this verse. But the person who is poor, who must daily seek for food, for water that is safe, for clothes to wear—the homeless person in our cities, the very poor around the world—for them these immediate concerns are a matter of life and death. How can they give up the search for daily food or for warm clothes in the winter? Are they being faithless? Can the wealthier neighbors of the poor think of themselves as spiritually superior because they do not have to consider these daily needs with such earnestness?

What would matter for both groups, the economically secure and the poor, is to remember the conclusion of the passage in verse 33 where Jesus calls them to seek first the kingdom of God. That might be a common challenge to both groups. In fact, it could be a point at which they could find agreement. The kingdom includes justice so that all have enough. If both the rich and the poor are seeking the kingdom, there exists the possibility of equalizing the resources.

In most Protestant congregations in our society we rarely find extremes of economic levels. There may be some members with much greater wealth, but they are unlikely to be in the same congregation as the very poor. This means that whatever attitudes we have toward those of a very different economic group are not likely to surface within the life of the congregation. A study of this passage, looking at groups for whom it would be very difficult to ignore immediate needs, can aid in the understanding of the poor as well as in seeing how very difficult this passage could be. It could also cause a more economically privileged congregation to look at ways in which their concern for their own long-term security causes them to put the goals of the kingdom as a distant second to their own security. They may not be concerned for tomorrow, but they may well be concerned about a year, or ten years, or fifty years from now, and how secure their situation will be then. They may not be so different after all from the very poor who must worry about today and tomorrow.

METHODOLOGY

In the High Middle Ages, around the twelfth and thirteen centuries, a form of theology called "scholasticism" developed in the newly created universities. There is much to oppose in the scholastic way of doing theology, but there is also some great strength. The scholastic argument was really a debate, raising all the objections that could be imagined about the position the theologian was going to take. These objections could be on the basis of the Bible, other church teachings, philosophers, or common sense. After listing the strongest arguments against their own position, theologians then outlined their own understanding. Finally, they returned to the original opposing statements, showing how such opinions were not the best interpretation.

To apply a scholastic method to sermon preparation—preparation, not delivery—would mean listing, at least mentally, all of the reasons members of a congregation might see what the preacher is saying as wrong or insignificant. It means that the preacher needs to do some homework on a variety of biblical passages that impinge, challenge, or clarify the text that has been chosen. It means following trails that the text gives us to other parts of Scripture. These can be passages that are alluded to in the chosen passage, or texts we think of that challenge or parallel it in some way. This is true for a variety of reasons. First, when the congregation may well be hesitant to accept the teaching precisely because it goes against the accepted wisdom of our society, it is helpful for the preacher to be able to draw on more than one passage and show that this teaching is at the heart of the whole biblical message. Second, looking at all of these different but related passages helps the preacher better understand what the passage means.

The biblical authors drew on the sacred texts they had at their disposal. The prophets drew on the law; the New Testament authors drew on the Old Testament; later parts of the New Testament drew on the earlier sections or on the oral tradition circulating in the churches. Therefore when we approach a particular text, we need to consider the texts the author also had in mind and knew the audience already understood. Words like "daily bread" or "vengeance" take on new meaning for us when we study other texts that use such terms. This does not oppose the historical-critical method that seeks to understand each text in its own uniqueness, but it does seek to find deeper meaning in the wider biblical witness.

How can this be done? It requires that the preacher be immersed in scripture—in the whole of Scripture. When a particular passage is read, what other passages come to mind? Which reinforce the text? Which go in another direction or really oppose it? What arguments from common sense relate to this? What arguments from a general knowledge of the Christian faith support or oppose it? This is not topical preaching, as though there were an issue the preacher wished to deal with and then sought out texts for this purpose. Rather, it is textual preaching, but with the realization that when the text appears to be difficult it is necessary to look at what issues within our culture are making it so. That can lead to preaching on an issue, but it is based on a particular text. Whether the text comes from the lectionary or from the preacher's own choosing, biblical passages that are difficult can be helpfully approached in this manner.

Therefore our method in the next five chapters will be to present a text, then to discuss why this text is difficult in our contemporary society. Next we will explore briefly other biblical voices that relate to the chosen text. This will be followed by a deeper study of the text itself. Finally, there will be some brief suggestions as to how the sermon could be developed. In the final chapter, there will be a discussion of the actual preaching event itself, including the full development of one of the texts previously studied.

CHAPTER ONE

Can the Consumer Ever Be Satisfied?

THE TEXT

Proverbs 30:7-9

> Two things I ask of you;
>   do not deny them to me before I die;
> Remove far from me falsehood and lying;
>   give me neither poverty nor riches;
>   feed me with the food that I need,
> or I shall be full, and deny you,
>   and say, "Who is the LORD?"
> or I shall be poor, and steal,
>   and profane the name of my God.

THE DIFFICULTY

We live in a consumer-driven society. No one can doubt that, and no one is immune. Advertising thrives because we must constantly be made to feel that we need more and more—the latest, the best. Our economy is fed by our own increasing sense of need. If we felt we did not need any more things, if we believed that what we already had was enough, then somehow the whole economic machinery would come crashing down and we would have nothing. That at least is what we are led to believe.

Capitalism has discovered an engine of great productivity and innovation. It has fostered aggressive development, often with enormous advancement in human health and comfort. Is this productivity necessarily based on greed, or can there be such productivity without greed, with a sense of sufficiency and generosity? Can there be generosity that does not foster dependency, but increases in others their own productivity and creativity? These are societal questions that Christians really need to study and explore. Such study would require more resources than most congregations have, and would involve lengthy and serious work with economists and others. Such study is not to be either underestimated or ignored. Christians need to find ways of raising these questions and demanding answers in the midst of the wider society, even if we do not have the answers already ourselves. There are others of goodwill outside the church who are also concerned, and we should work with them.

Unlike traditional societies where one generation lives very much as did their ancestors a century before, in our own society we live in the midst of constant newness. New inventions, new gadgets, appear on the horizon every day. For many people, the desire to be among the first to have the newest is more of a goad to consumption than it is the fear of scarcity. Advertising aids and abets this desire as well. Especially among children and teenagers, the fear of not having that which has been declared "in" can become traumatic. There is obviously a felt need, but is it a true need or an artificially stimulated one?

This is not to say that all new inventions, or what might even be termed "gadgets," cannot be answers to true need. Think of the developments in communications technology over the past few decades. There has been a revolution that has made it possible for people to communicate quickly around the world. Even in areas of the world where putting up telephone lines would take years, satellite cell phones now can be used without such expensive infrastructure. Families can keep in touch, disasters can be reported and aid rendered; the world has been made smaller. Cell phones used by passengers on the hijacked planes on September 11 limited the terrible damage that was done.

The latest and newest, however, are not always needed the moment they appear on the scene. We can imagine parents asking a ten-year-old to wait six months without the absolutely necessary sports shoes of the latest fashion, precisely to show the child that by the time the six months is up these shoes will no longer be the item that is absolutely needed. Something else will have been declared "in" at that point. We also can imagine the ten-year-old turning the tables on the parents about a new computer or cell phone. We are all subject to the same pressures to consume.

In the midst of this culture, two questions beg to be asked. The first: Is there not enough real need in the world—indeed in our own country—so that the economic dynamo we live in could be sustained by meeting these needs instead of the artificially stimulated ones that advertising seeks to create? Could there not be a mechanism found so that those who are truly in need could develop the resources to acquire what they lack? The second question is quite different: Are Christians called to have a sense of "enough," of limit, of sufficiency, even in the midst of a culture that always desires to have us want more?

We can reverse the two questions and ask: If we were satisfied with "enough," would we then find creative ways of directing now surplus goods and services into the places where there truly is need? Could it be used to help others become nondependent and contributing members of the society? Could it help those who must be dependent—for instance, the sick, the elderly—have lives of dignity?

Scripture constantly links generosity and sufficiency. If we are frugal but not generous, the problem of others' needs is not answered. That is the stance of the miser. It is very difficult to talk about stewardship if there is no sense of enough. Stewardship is not easy when people feel they are truly depriving themselves or their families of necessities. If they already have a sense that their own real needs are met, then there can be greater generosity with what remains.

Of course we have responsibilities to provide what is needed for ourselves and our families. That is not questioned. Often the poorest are more generous than the well-to-do, however. Perhaps the poor have developed a greater knowledge of what is truly necessary because of their own poverty, or perhaps they have been forced to live outside a consumer mentality and have learned to live on different terms.

For many in our culture, however, it is as though we have lost any inner sense of what is enough. There is no stopping point that we can find for ourselves, other than the decision that we cannot afford something. Even in that case, the enormous credit debt with which some of us have burdened ourselves shows that, for many, affordability is not a barrier to consumption.

Rather than looking at the much discussed issue of the imbalance of wealth and poverty in our world, which is indeed an overwhelmingly significant issue, let us look at the more personal and theological question: Were we created by God to be able to tell when we have enough—enough food, enough clothing, enough money, enough housing, enough of anything and everything? Is part of our sinful condition the fact that we no longer have such a sense? Is part of the meaning of redemption a regaining of this ability to find a stopping point? It would be far easier for us to deal with the question of what to do with a surplus we accumulate when we know that we have enough. The issue of wealth and poverty in our world is an issue of justice, and it must be faced. The question of "enough," however, is also a theological question. It is a matter of what we were created to be. It has the advantage of being a question we can wrestle with as individuals, as families, and as congregations. We do not have to wait for economists and those skilled in international relations or politics to begin our work.

OTHER BIBLICAL VOICES

(1) Ezekiel 34:1-31

In these verses, the prophet gives a description of his society as God sees it. He compares the people to a flock of sheep, some strong and some weak. The strong push away the weak from the needed water and pasture so that the weak become even weaker. The strong sheep even destroy what they do not need.

> Is it not enough for you to feed on the good pasture, but you must tread down with your feet the rest of your pasture? When you drink of clear water, must you foul the rest with your feet? And

must my sheep eat what you have trodden with your feet, and drink what you have fouled with your feet? (Ezekiel 34:18-19)

What is implied throughout this passage is that God has provided enough pasture and water for the whole flock. But because the strong not only take what they need but also destroy what they do not need, the weak are unable to meet their own needs. It is not only greed, but unnecessary destruction of resources that has caused shortages. What this means is that not only must we have a sense of the limits of our own needs, but also we must be concerned that in meeting our needs we do not destroy that which would meet the needs of others. This scarcity is artificially created by the strong who have taken what they wished without regard for the needs of others. How we organize our economic life must take into account not only meeting our own needs but also preserving what we do not use so that the needs of others can be met. Whether we consider the concern of weaker nations in our world today or weaker communities within our own nation, or whether we consider the needs of future generations, we cannot escape the challenge to use wisely and responsibly the resources at our disposal so that others who are not as strong may also meet their own needs. Whether it is ways of removing coal without destroying farmland, conducting commercial fishing without destroying future catches, or creating chemical plants that do not contaminate water supplies, the issue of the strong needing to be careful for the sake of the weak remains one that Christians must always consider.

Ezekiel places the blame for the situation he describes not only on the strong sheep but also on the political and religious leaders—the shepherds of the people—who have failed in their responsibility to see that the needs of all, the weak as well as the strong, are met. He writes: "Ah, you shepherds of Israel who have been feeding yourselves!... You have not strengthened the weak, you have not healed the sick, you have not bound up the injured, you have not brought back the strayed, you have not sought the lost, but with force and harshness you have ruled them" (Ezekiel 34:2, 4). It was the task of the shepherds to see that the resources were wisely used, that the strong did not destroy what they did not use, and that the weak received what they needed.

It is interesting that the prophet, speaking for God, does not first of all blame the sheep, but the shepherds. There is both comfort and challenge for us in this. There is comfort in the fact that, as ordinary citizens, we know that there is not a great deal we can do about some injustices. They go far beyond the scope of our powers or abilities to change. We have all heard stories of the child who is told by his mother to finish his dinner. "Think of all the starving people in Africa," the mother says. The child replies: "Take these vegetables and send them to Africa." We know the solution is not so easy. Cutting down on our own consumption individually probably will do nothing to alter the international situation. We cannot simply send our dinner there.

On one hand, to blame those in power, the political and governmental structures, does seem to ease our own personal responsibility. On the other hand, we live in a democracy. We are to some degree at least responsible for the government we have. We elect the officials. We live in a society where we can organize, we can petition, we can speak out. Therefore we cannot absolve ourselves of all responsibility. Giving up on the political process because we doubt that it would make any difference puts us in the camp of the guilty shepherds.

One of the problems we face at the moment, however, is deciding who the contemporary "shepherds" really are. In Ezekiel's time, it was clear that he meant the king and the priests. They were the ones placed by God to govern the people. It was a religious state, with king and priests sharing in the ruling power. Who are our shepherds? For the whole people of our nation we cannot merely point to the religious leaders of any particular group, though surely we can say that all of them have some responsibility to help their own congregations understand the wider issues of the nation and the responsibilities of citizens. We can assume that the political powers—executive, judicial, and legislative branches at all levels, from local to national—have the character of shepherds of the people. Though elected by the people rather than inheriting office as in ancient Israel, most public leaders at least speak of their sense of responsibility for the welfare of all the people.

However, much of the actual decision-making power in our world is not wielded by the governments of individual nations. Much is exercised by commercial interests that go beyond a single nation. If we consider weak nations and strong nations rather than the weak and strong communities within our own country, then it is not clear that there are any shepherds at all. How are we to deal with this issue? Especially as part of a strong nation, what is our responsibility to weak nations? Ought there to be "shepherds," structures that are charged with making sure the strong nations do not take advantage of the weak? Can this be done democratically? For many people, including many within our churches, nationalism is a religious duty. Much of the religious opposition to the United Nations is based on a fear of losing national sovereignty. Fear of global government, of some "new international world order" has spawned dozens of conspiracy theories. How are we as citizens to balance national interests and the realities of international injustice? When we say in the creed that we believe in "the one, holy, catholic church," we affirm that, as the church, we are part of a global reality of the body of Christ. Somehow that reality should help us see beyond our own national interests. These are critical issues to which we are called to respond. Though ancient Israel often equated the nation with the people of God, we cannot. The church, the people of God, extends far beyond any national borders. The government of a single nation cannot be the shepherd of all, and yet the church understands the need for shepherds, those responsible for the welfare of the whole people.

The prophet Ezekiel goes on to give the description of what will happen when God's redemption comes, when God will indeed come among them as their shepherd. A true king after God's own heart will lead the people. Then the crops will flourish and there will be no more hunger. It is greed and wanton destruction that cause scarcity. When these are ended, then there will be plenty for all. In the meantime, all who have a shepherd-like responsibility, including religious leaders, have a duty to help the strong sheep understand the limits they must observe.

(2) Matthew 6:25-33

This passage is part of the Sermon on the Mount and contains the famous words about not being concerned about what we eat or drink or wear. We often read this passage as though it were saying such issues are unimportant because they are merely physical needs, whereas we should be concerned about spiritual matters.

This is clearly not what the passage means. In fact, in verse 32 we read: "For it is the Gentiles who strive for all these things; and indeed your heavenly Father knows that you need all these things."

Food, clothing, shelter—these are basic to human life. All humanity needs these things. They are so important that God is concerned about them as well. God has created us to need food. Furthermore, God has provided it for us. We could argue that God did not create us to need clothing, for in Genesis 3:7 the need to hide one's nakedness is the result of sin. But in Genesis 3:21 it is God who gives Adam and Eve proper clothes for their new, post-Eden life. However we deal with these accounts of creation, it is clear that God continues to provide what God's own creatures need. So we cannot assume that food and water, shelter and clothing are unimportant issues. What Matthew 6:32 implies is that they are very important matters, so important that God is concerned about them. Based on the fact that God is taking care of these basic provisions, our first task is to pursue righteousness, to strive for the kingdom of God, to order our lives now in accord with the goals of the kingdom.

If we look at this passage in the light of Ezekiel 34, then we can see even more clearly the connections between having our basic needs met and pursuing righteousness. God has provided enough for all of us to have the food, the clothing, the shelter, the water that we need. The fact that some do not have enough of these things has to do with the fact that there is unrighteousness, injustice, wanton destruction, and misuse of resources, all of which lead to the maldistribution we now see. The way to make sure all have enough is to seek righteousness first. The kingdom of God is concerned with such matters as food and clothing. In that kingdom, there will be enough for all, precisely because justice and righteousness will prevail. Justice and righteousness are not two separate issues. Matthew uses the term "righteousness" to mean fulfilling the will of God. It is to live now as if in the kingdom, where God's will is totally obeyed.[1]

The very basic issue Christians must consider is whether it is true that there really is enough food, water, and materials for shelter and clothing in God's creation for all of us. Obviously, if what some of us demand is two or three houses, more than enough clothing, wasteful use of water, and means of production that are destructive, then there may not be enough. If we have no sense of enough, then there may not be enough in God's creation for all of us. However, if there really is enough given by God in creation for all of us, then something is radically wrong when many do not have their basic needs met. The cure is to seek first the kingdom of God and righteousness. Then all the rest—the food, the clothing— will indeed be given not only to us, but to all people. Ambrose, bishop of Milan in the late-fourth century, wrote:

> [N]ature has poured forth all things for all men for common use. God has ordered all things to be produced, so that there should be food in common to all, and that the earth should be a common possession for all. Nature, therefore, has produced a common right for all, but greed has made it a right for a few.[2]

(3) Ecclesiastes 9:7-9

The whole book of Ecclesiastes is often viewed as extremely pessimistic. It is written by one who is, at the most, agnostic about any life after death. The author also holds that the law of God provides guidance for the good life here and now; and there is indeed judgment by God, though exactly how or when that judgment comes is not known.

The book is realistic about this life, however. Those who are good are not always rewarded, nor are the evil always punished. Bad things do happen to good people. In the midst of this realism, however, there is the word of how to lead the good life:

> Go, eat your bread with enjoyment, and drink your wine with a merry heart; for God has long ago approved what you do. Let your garments always be white; do not let oil be lacking on your head. Enjoy life with the wife whom you love, all the days of your vain life that are given you under the sun, because that is your portion in life and in your toil at which you toil under the sun.

It is not possessions themselves that give enjoyment, for there are those who possess much and yet are dissatisfied and always seek more. Enjoyment, satisfaction, a sense of fulfillment, true joy— these are not something that possessions can give. Such joy is a gift of God.[3] Joy is what we should seek. Granted, joy would be very difficult in a situation of extreme poverty and deprivation. But for most of us, the problem is the lack of joy, the lack of a sense of enough in what we do possess, so that our life is governed by seeking more rather than in the quiet enjoyment, the generosity of spirit and of goods, that what we already possess could make possible. Such joy is not something we can create for ourselves. Rather, it is the gift of God. It is a graceful attitude. It is what Ecclesiastes views as true wisdom: "There is nothing better for mortals than to eat and drink, and find enjoyment in their toil. This also, I saw, is from the hand of God; for apart from him who can eat or who can have enjoyment? For to the one who pleases him God gives wisdom and knowledge and joy" (2:24-26a).

If any word typifies Ecclesiastes, it is "enough." Be satisfied with what you have. Be content with the simple pleasures God has provided for human life. Granted, there is misery. There is poverty. There is illness. Part of our task is to be generous, righteous, and merciful, and to be a friend to others. That is stressed throughout. In fact, the opposite of wise living is always seeking for more, never being satisfied with "enough": "Again, I saw vanity under the sun: the case of solitary individuals, without sons or brothers; yet there is no end to all their toil, and their eyes are never satisfied with riches" (4:7-8c). In contrast, the wise person rejoices in family and friends, and is satisfied with what God has given to that person. Even a strong belief in the resurrection of the dead does not negate the truth of this realism.

"What God has given us" was probably more obvious in a traditional society than it is in ours. In a traditional society, the next generation probably lived in the same house, farmed the same land as did the previous generations. In that society, satisfaction would be defined by simple acceptance of what one had received. Our situation is quite different. We do not generally inherit our wealth in land and livestock. What our parents gave us was probably the opportunity for education, with the expectation that we could then earn our own living. These words cannot mean that the person in our society who is born very poor should remain there. Nor do we remain in the same houses or even in the same communities. How we calculate "enough" in our situation is an important and a difficult question.

Ecclesiastes is not alone in this concern for contentment with what we have. In 1 Timothy 6:6-10 we find the same sentiments combined with a very familiar verse:

> Of course, there is great gain in godliness combined with contentment; for we brought nothing into the world, so that we can take nothing out of it; but if we have food and clothing, we will be content with these. But those who want to be rich fall into temptation and are trapped by many senseless and harmful desires that plunge people into ruin and destruction. For the love of money is a root of all kinds of evil, and in their eagerness to be rich some have wandered away from the faith and pierced themselves with many pains.

Contentment with enough. That is a sense that is worth rediscovering in our society. In this context, "the love of money is a root of all kinds of evil."

Of course there must be enough to meet basic human requirements. The issue is the lack of contentment with enough, so that our lives are geared to gaining more. Contentment and enjoyment then never come. Let me give a mundane example of this. My parents both loved good coffee. To them, good coffee meant well-brewed with real cream and sugar. During World War II, they gave up their cream and sugar "for the duration" because these were scarce items. All the time they regretted that they did not have the coffee they loved, the coffee they really could enjoy. As soon as the war ended, they prepared cream and sugar, ceremoniously brewed coffee and were ready finally to have the coffee for which they had been yearning. With the first sip, they both realized that their tastes had changed. They did not like coffee with cream and sugar anymore. So with fresh cups, they drank their coffee black with no sugar, and enjoyed it. They laughed at this, because obviously they could have enjoyed their coffee throughout the war. But because they were convinced they could only enjoy it with what they did not yet have, they missed the contentment that was possible. Their tastes had changed long before the war ended, but they did not know it. And when they finally could have what they had longed for, it did not bring the enjoyment they had anticipated.

Many of us live our lives assuming we really could be content if only we had something we have yet to acquire or achieve.

Meanwhile, we overlook the contentment that could really be ours if only we had been open to it. If and when we finally attain what we long for, we may well find it brings no more contentment than we had, and may spur us on to the next level of what we really think we need in order to be satisfied. It can be a never-ending search. Ecclesiastes points to the ability to enjoy what we already have as a gift of God. First Timothy points to exactly the same thing. Somehow godliness and contentment go together. A lack of contentment can lead to wandering away from the faith in search of the "more" we feel we need. Paul's faith was obviously strong. He had the gift Ecclesiastes looks for—the gift of being satisfied. He writes to the Philippians: "I have learned to be content with whatever I have. I know what it is to have little, and I know what it is to have plenty" (Philippians 4:11*b*-12*a*).

(4) Deuteronomy 14:22-26

This passage in Deuteronomy is usually overlooked when we think about the ancient law of tithing. We assume the whole tithe was somehow given to God through the priests for the use of the priests and the poor. That was indeed the case every third year. But in the other years it was different:

> Set apart a tithe of all the yield of your seed that is brought in yearly from the field. In the presence of the LORD your God, in the place that he will choose as a dwelling for his name, you shall eat the tithe of your grain, your wine, and your oil, as well as the firstlings of your herd and flock, so that you may learn to fear the LORD your God always. But if, when the LORD your God has blessed you, the distance is so great that you are unable to transport it, because the place where the LORD your God will choose to set his name is too far away from you, then you may turn it into money. With the money secure in hand, go to the place that the LORD your God will choose; spend the money for whatever you wish—oxen, sheep, wine, strong drink, or whatever you desire. And you shall eat there in the presence of the LORD your God, you and your household rejoicing together. (Deuteronomy 14:22-26)

Obviously, the God of Israel and of the church is not opposed to enjoyment and feasting. Even in the midst of a simple lifestyle, there must be times of such joyful abundance. What is commanded here in Deuteronomy is not only for good times. Even if the harvest is small, such celebrations were to occur every third year. Nor was the celebration only for the rich. It was a command for all the families of Israel.

The stress on eating and drinking with enjoyment may seem strange to us, almost hedonistic. But it should not. At the heart of both Judaism and Christianity is the joy in meals that are part of worship. Whether it is Passover or the Sabbath meal in Israel, or the Lord's Supper in Christianity, there is something sacred about feasting. We are rejoicing in God's good gifts to us. The eating and drinking with enjoyment that Ecclesiastes and these other passages urge is not a solitary endeavor. Rather, it is a joyful meal with others in God's presence. People who lack wisdom are viewed much more as solitary, or as unable to sit and enjoy such a feast without seeing if they are better than others, or if they are wasting a feast on those who cannot do them any good. Charles Dickens, in *A Christmas Carol*, points to the difference between the solitary Scrooge who finds feasting and celebrating a waste, and the poor Cratchett family that, even with little, is able to enjoy the feast. Scrooge's redemption involved learning to be part of such feasting.

The early church met daily for common meals—"love feasts"—as well as for the Lord's Supper. These love feasts were real meals, as the Lord's Supper originally had been. They were joyful meals. We have lost something when we think of the Lord's Supper as so solemn it is no longer festive, or as individual rather than communal. In a highly individualistic society that is even losing the habit of family meals, we can learn much from the wisdom of Ecclesiastes and these other witnesses. In the Eucharist we celebrate that what Jesus Christ has done for our salvation is "enough." In all of our meals we celebrate that what God has given us is "enough." Ecclesiastes calls us to celebrate "enough."

BACK TO THE TEXT: PROVERBS 30:7-9

The text from Proverbs is not a particularly famous passage. Few of us have it memorized like that part of the Sermon on the Mount about food and clothing. Yet this passage fully captures the issue of "enough." It speaks of the dangers of having too much as well as having too little. It combines the desire to have just enough with the desire to know and speak the truth. These are the two requests of God, the sum total of what the writer hopes he can have before he dies.

Several things are interesting about this passage. First, it is clear that the writer assumes that only God can provide these things. Only God can let us see and speak the truth. Left to ourselves we can readily believe what is to our benefit and deny the truth of unpleasant realities that would challenge us. It is precisely this truthfulness that the writer desires. It is a truthfulness that would really let us know when we have enough and when we do not. Such knowledge is not within our own power, precisely because of human sin. This means that if we wish such ability, then we must pray for it. Such knowledge is part of the process of redemption, a part that we usually do not consider.

Second, the request is that God will feed us with the food we need. Such a petition reinforces the fact that God is the ultimate source of all we need for our lives. "The food that I need" does not refer to the type of food, but to the amount. The phrase is found in a few other places in Scripture. In Exodus 16:16-18, the Israelites in the wilderness were given directions concerning the gathering of the miraculous manna. The head of each household was commanded to gather a certain amount—about a quart—for each person in the tent. The text reads: " 'Gather as much of it as each of you needs, an omer to a person.' " The phrase "as much as each of you needs" is the same as in Proverbs 30:8—"the food that I need." The phrase really means the amount deemed necessary for a day—"the bread of my portion," or, as in the New International Version, "my daily bread."[4] However, in the Exodus story, some gathered more than they should have, and the rest had too little. A further miracle occurred. When each family measured the amount they had, the "too much" and the "too little" had both been corrected to the exact amount each person needed. The right amount is enough. All else is too much or too little.

What is interesting about the Exodus passage is that it took a miracle to overcome the tendency to gather more than what was needed. God had given clear directions here as to what was enough, but they were not heeded. In order to preserve the new covenant community on the path it should go, a miraculous redistribution occurred.

Paul quoted this passage when he wrote to the Corinthian church concerning their support for the Jerusalem church. In 2 Corinthians 8:8-15, he refers to the miraculous distribution as the goal Christians should have. If Corinth at the moment has more than it needs and Jerusalem has less, then Corinth should voluntarily carry out what it took a miracle to do during the Exodus. After all, they, the church, are the community of the Holy Spirit. They are the body of Christ. In a sense, the church is already a miraculous community, and therefore it should be within its power to do the proper distribution.

Finally, the phrase "my daily bread," or "my proper portion," obviously is part of the Lord's Prayer. There is every reason to assume that Jesus and the early Jewish-Christian church were well aware of this phrase in Exodus and in Proverbs. When we as Christians pray this prayer, we usually do not imagine that we are asking not only that there will be enough of what we need, but also that there will not be too much. Perhaps if we were aware of this meaning we would not pray it so glibly! But the words do mean that, as our wider biblical context has demonstrated.

The author of Proverbs is well aware of the dangers of both too much and too little. On the one hand, those who have too much can easily assume that it is their own ability that has gained what they have, and therefore they need not bother about God. On the other hand, the community of faith is to be an exemplary moral witness; and if the poor need to steal in order to eat, then that is a profanation of God's name and the witness the community is to make. This is not saying that it is better for a poor person to starve to death than to steal, but rather that if in dire straits a poor person must steal in order to live, then that still remains a profanation. It shows that the community, and not only the poor person, is not living the way God intended.

Can we imagine for whom or for what community this passage from Proverbs would not be a challenge but rather a great comfort? Neither the rich nor the poor can automatically fit this category, for both have their difficulties. The rich are obviously in danger of always seeking more, or of trusting their possessions rather than God. The poor are in a different situation. There are places in today's world where the economic system is in such chaos that many people simply do not have enough to survive. This is sometimes the result of the collapse of one economic system and the slow progress toward a new one. The people are working hard, but paychecks do not come, or else the pay is so small that it does not even provide for the most basic of needs. A whole culture of stealing develops—stealing from the government, from work—to have something to sell on the black market in order to survive or have something to feed one's family. But though stealing might be condoned as a last resort in such a situation—and this passage understands that it might come to that—it still is opposed to God's will for humanity. The poor in such a situation also have the difficult task of determining what is enough, even if supported by stealing.

There have been people who learned the truth of this passage the hard way. Think of those who had all sorts of riches because of their celebrity status or by means of illegal activities. They had enormous sums of money, but they discovered that money did not bring joy. In their despair they turned to drugs or alcohol, or their illegal activities caught up with them. They lost their money, but in the midst of their financial loss they found a new life. Not all do, but these people did, often through a new or rekindled faith. In this new life, there was a sense of enough. There was a sense that the simple joys of friends and family, of significant work that contributes to others, of generosity, are what make life meaningful. Perhaps they once disregarded God in the pride of their wealth. Now they know wealth can disappear in a moment. Whatever they have is a gift, and, if they are blessed, they will also have the most important gift of being able to find joy in what has been given to them without seeking for more. For many people in this country, the events of September 11 led to such a re-evaluation of what is truly important.

This prayer in Proverbs is asking for what the passage in Ecclesiastes points to as the key to the good life: the ability to know when one has enough, and to receive it as a gift of God to be enjoyed. It is a truth the church needs to emphasize especially to those of us who consume without thought, following the siren song of the advertisers.

This may be a difficult truth to preach if the church itself does not practice it, especially at the congregational level. In fact, that may be a place to begin. If a congregation can learn what is enough, it may then have the freedom to use what is more than enough for the good of others. To the households within the congregation it may also be a witness of the joy that can come with such contentment that is the gift of God.

Preaching This Text Today

This text from Proverbs could be useful as the beginning of a stewardship season. The central theme would be the relationship of stewardship and knowing that we have enough. Relating it first to the life of the congregation might make it easier to relate the concept to individuals or families.

How does a congregation know if it has enough—enough budget, enough staff, enough space? Does it always seem that more would be better? If there were enough for the congregation, what could be done with what was left over? If there were not enough, what exactly is missing? From there the preacher could point to the effects of sin on our ability to know when we do have enough.

It might be helpful to look first at the known words—the phrase from the Lord's Prayer, "our daily bread." The question could be asked, What did Jesus and the first disciples understand this to mean? The preacher could then make brief reference to the Exodus story, and then deal with the Proverbs text in greater detail. It should be emphasized that the Proverbs text shows that by ourselves we cannot tell what is enough. Sin has robbed us of that ability. Rather, we need the self-knowledge that only God can give. The preacher could also point to the fact that such self-knowledge is part of the meaning of redemption and is evidence of the attempt to overcome the effects of sin in our lives. To pray the Lord's Prayer means asking that we be given enough, and not too much or too little.

The conclusion could show that sin affects not only individuals, but also congregations. The stewardship season might well be a time for all of us, individual families as well as the congregation as a whole, to look at what we do have, on what basis we decide we need more, and what we could do with our resources if we decided we did have enough already. We could learn to pray earnestly that such knowledge would be given to us. If this text were used at the beginning of the stewardship season, other passages mentioned above, especially from Ezekiel and Deuteronomy, might follow as sermons on the next Sundays.

SUGGESTED READING

Clifford, Richard J. *Proverbs: A Commentary.* Louisville: Westminster/John Knox Press, 1999.

Farmer, Kathleen A. *Who Knows What Is Good? A Commentary on the Books of Proverbs and Ecclesiastes.* International Theological Commentary. Grand Rapids: Wm. B. Eerdmans Publishing Co., 1991.

Perdue, Leo G. *Proverbs.* Interpretation: A Bible Commentary for Teaching and Preaching. Louisville: John Knox Press, 2000.

CHAPTER TWO

Celibacy? You're Kidding!

THE TEXT

1 Corinthians 7:1-8, 25-28

Now concerning the matters about which you wrote: "It is well for a man not to touch a woman." But because of cases of sexual immorality, each man should have his own wife and each woman her own husband. The husband should give to his wife her conjugal rights, and likewise the wife to her husband. For the wife does not have authority over her own body, but the husband does; likewise the husband does not have authority over his own body, but the wife does. Do not deprive one another except perhaps by agreement for a set time, to devote yourselves to prayer, and then come together again, so that Satan my not tempt you because of your lack of self-control. This I say by way of concession, not of command. I wish that all were as I myself am. But each has a particular gift from God, one having one kind and another a different kind.

To the unmarried and the widows I say that it is well for them to remain unmarried as I am....

Now concerning virgins, I have no command of the Lord, but I give my opinion as one who by the Lord's mercy is trustworthy. I think that, in view of the impending crisis, it is well for you to remain as you are. Are you bound to a wife? Do not seek to be free. Are you free from a wife? Do not seek a wife. But if you marry, you do not sin, and if a virgin marries, she does not sin. Yet those who marry will experience distress in this life, and I would spare you that.

THE DIFFICULTY

For anyone who has lived more than fifty years, the changes in our culture in the area of sexuality are astonishing. What once was assumed to be absolutely prohibited in public—in movies, billboards, general magazines, television, and so forth—now is so commonplace as to be unremarkable. What once would have been labeled as "adult" or "X-rated" now is to be seen almost any time and place. Where once even the mention of pregnancy could lead to dismissal from broadcasting, now the most intimate details of someone's unusual sex life are matters for daytime talk shows. In advertising, sex is used to sell everything from cars to sneakers.

What we often term the sexual revolution took shape in the 1960s, and to some degree has been with us ever since. It was not simply a change in attitudes. It was also the result of the discovery of a simple method of contraception that women could control. This is the famous "pill." Combined with the developing feminist movement, the pill gave women new control over pregnancy. It permitted them to combine marriage and education, as well as marriage and career plans. Single women needed no longer to fear pregnancy if they were to lead an active sexual life. It did not take long for this possibility of sexual freedom for women to be publicly acknowledged (perhaps pushed by men) and, to some degree, made acceptable. Even in the face of later concerns about the pill and AIDS, behavior has not altered very much.

Even many early adolescents now assume sexual freedom. For the past several decades, especially among a significant group of younger people, sex has almost been considered a sport: find someone else who likes to play, and there is no reason not to. Sex has become a leisure-time activity, in many ways severed from any serious, intimate, interpersonal involvement. One does not need such involvement to play tennis, another sport that it takes two to play, and for many people sex has become very much like that.

What does the church have to say to these present realities? Often churches assume that it is only other people's unmarried children who have active sex lives. Therefore churches continue simply to condemn such behavior, or else they refuse to discuss the matter at all.

Young people do face serious decisions. They always have. But the changes in the culture discussed above make the situation even more difficult now. Young people are surrounded by sexually explicit messages. Movies and television show a lifestyle in which constant sexual activity is seen as normal and expected. Where once the social pressure on women, especially young women, was toward virginity until marriage, now much peer pressure is against it. At the same time, in an economy that requires more and more education, the period of adolescence has been extended.

It is not only today's young people who are affected by this cultural change. The young people of the 1960s are now probably grandparents. The majority of our population has grown up in the midst of this sexually explicit context. Whether we agree with it or not, all of us have to deal with it.

With these issues in mind, we will look at some biblical passages that deal with human sexuality in general, and marriage in particular.

OTHER BIBLICAL VOICES

(1) The Song of Solomon

Perhaps the most famous section of the Bible on the subject of human sexuality is the Song of Solomon. It is clearly a love song, and a rather sensual one at that. The explicit character of its imagery has led many religious leaders, both in Judaism and in Christianity, to assume that the poem is really an allegory of the love between God and Israel, between Christ and the church, or between God and the individual soul, since courtship and marriage imagery for God and the people is found in many places in Scripture. At least if it were an allegory, that would account for its inclusion in Scripture, because on its face it has little to do with the usual concerns of the Bible. It does not mention God. It does mention King Solomon and Jerusalem. What is clear is that even if it is viewed as an allegory, the beauty of human love and attraction between a man and a woman is extolled. The whole poem may be a royal marriage song, and one might assume that children will be the hoped-for result of such a marriage. But there is no mention of children as the purpose of this love.

(2) Genesis 1:26–2:24; 24:67

The early chapters of Genesis present two different accounts of the creation of human beings. If we had only the Genesis 1 version, we would assume that humans were created as sexual beings for the purpose of procreation. Procreation is very prominent in this story. As soon as they are created they are commanded "to be fruitful and multiply." There is no sense here that only two persons, one male and one female, have been created and given this command. There could have been several couples, just as the preceding verses give no sense that only one pair of each kind of animal was created. But no matter how many human pairs were created at the beginning, high priority in this version is given to procreation.

For centuries the church generally agreed with this understanding and saw children as the major, if not the sole, purpose of marriage. Part of this was the economic need for children in order to increase the size of the nation, to care for elderly parents, or to work on the farm. It also was a time of underpopulation in most areas. Even in recent years, within the Roman Catholic Church, discussions of the legitimacy of contraceptives by a married couple have been based largely on the view that procreation is the main if not the sole reason for marriage and for sexual relations.

The demographic situation has changed drastically in our own time, especially in industrialized societies. Overpopulation rather than underpopulation is our concern. In a modern industrial or post-industrial society, children are an expense rather than an economic benefit, since they must be educated and they do not work as part of the family economic unit when they are five or six years old. Children now are usually supported by their parents until they are at least eighteen, and perhaps, because of expensive higher education, beyond that. When they finally are employed, it is not anticipated that they will be supporting their parents. With pension plans, Social Security, and so forth, parents do not generally expect to be supported financially by their children. In the non-industrial world where parents assume they need many children in order to have a few survive to take care of them in their old age, dramatic improvements in infant mortality, because of modern medicine, mean that more children survive than would have been expected a century ago. This leads to a different set of problems that such a society is not prepared for: enormous increases in population, lack of employment, and increased poverty.

Genesis 2 presents us with a different account from the version in Genesis 1. First of all, there is only one couple. (We are so accustomed to this version that we read back into chapter 1 the idea that there was only one man and one woman in the beginning.) The man is created first, and it is clear to God that "It is not good that the man should be alone" (Genesis 2:18). All the animals were created, but none was an appropriate companion. Not until God created woman out of the man was there a suitable mate. She was different from the man, but he recognized in her a similarity to himself. Their sexual distinction appears in this story to be for the sake of companionship and not only for procreation. The man cried, "This at last is bone of my bones and flesh of my flesh" (Genesis 2:23). The passage concludes with the famous words: "Therefore a man leaves his father and his mother and clings to his wife, and they become one flesh" (Genesis 2:24). Their becoming one flesh points to the sexual union of the two, but procreation is not mentioned until later in the story.

According to this second creation story, no child is conceived before the fall. That is not to say that had there been no sin there would have been no children. But the actual conception of children is not discussed until the end of chapter 3. It is at that point that Adam names his wife Eve—"the mother of all living." Marriage in the earlier part of the story is above all for companionship, with children an important part, though they can be seen as the result of the parents' companionship rather than the cause of it. In this way, the account of Genesis 2 is an important addition to Genesis 1. It may well be that the priests who finally collected and brought together all the ancient writings put in both creation stories precisely because they correct or amplify one another in significant ways.

There is a vignette later in Genesis that picks up on the emphasis of Genesis 2. It is found in Genesis 24. After the death of Sarah, Abraham was very concerned about finding a proper wife for his son Isaac. Abraham sent a trusted servant back to his birthplace in order to seek a wife. The woman had to agree to come back with the servant. The servant did as commanded and found Rebekah. She agreed to come with him. When Isaac met her, he also believed that this was the woman he should marry. The chapter concludes with these words: "Then Isaac brought her into his mother Sarah's tent. He took Rebekah, and she became his wife; and he loved her. So Isaac was comforted after his mother's death" (Genesis 24:67).

The concluding sentence says much about the nature of the companionship of marriage. Families are very important. We grow up in a family, and yet it is to be expected that death will take away the parents of the family of origin. What marriage does is help to extend the old and create new families. Marriage is not just about two people. If all goes well, each partner acquires the sisters, brothers, and cousins of the mate. When there are children of this new marriage, the children have aunts and uncles and cousins on both sides of the family. Isaac was comforted not only because he had a wife, but also because he was forming a new part of the family. Even without children he was forming this new part. Children would add to it and push it into the next generation. Companionship and family are not separate issues.

Though there is this emphasis on companionship in marriage in the Bible, we cannot overlook the essential role of children. Marriage and procreation were almost a duty for everyone within Israel, and the inability of a woman to have children was seen both by her and the rest of the society as a terrible tragedy. The barren woman was socially unacceptable. If children were a blessing from God, then the lack of children was almost a curse. To perpetuate one's name, one's family line, was a form of immortality. It was contributing to the good of the tribe and of the nation.

Within the Old Testament, therefore, marriage is seen as the normative life for all people. There are no religious vows of celibacy, even though there are strict laws governing many aspects of sexuality. Marriage is expected for all. Children are the anticipated result, but there is also the clear message that human love and intimacy are values in themselves.

BACK TO THE TEXT: 1 CORINTHIANS 7:1-8, 25-28

It is obvious that there is a dramatic change from the Old Testament understanding to what we find in Paul's letter to the Corinthians. How much of a change and why requires a close reading of these strange and difficult words. Part of the difficulty is that these words about celibacy come to us through centuries of tradition. Beginning a few generations after Paul and continuing until modern times, this passage has been read as the justification for Christian monastic life in particular and for the superiority of celibacy over married life in general. It has been used to establish the negative character of human sexuality. The superior choice is to avoid it. Marriage is a lesser state, entered into only to avoid sin and to produce children. Though this may be the way in which Paul can be seen when looking back through the use of this text, a different picture emerges when we view Paul in his own context, the context of the Greco-Roman culture in which both he and the Corinthians lived.

The debate as to whether marriage was a help or a hindrance to the pursuit of wisdom was a common theme in the philosophy of the day, particularly the Stoic philosophy. Many of the arguments Paul uses would have been familiar to his audience. Jewish teachers before Paul had already used these arguments, adding their own Judaic interpretations. The basic debate was whether marriage brought more responsibilities and cares to a man and therefore prevented him from spending his time pursuing wisdom (or, in the case of Judaism, studying Torah), or whether a wife provided him with the support system that made such study possible. It was a common debate in the first century, and an entire body of literature had developed around the topic.[1]

It would appear that in Corinth some had taken the stance that marriage was a hindrance, and that even those who were married should now take on celibacy. A rather extreme sexual asceticism dominated at least part of the Corinthian church. Judging from some of his earlier writings to them, they may have expected Paul to take their side. Evidently they had written to Paul, asking a number of pointed questions about marriage and various issues associated with it.

In 7:1, scholars generally agree that Paul is quoting from their letter. It is the Corinthians, not Paul, who says: "It is well for a man not to touch a woman."[2] In fact, the rest of the chapter makes clear that this cannot be Paul's opinion, and he opposes the extreme opinions of the Corinthians. In 7:2-5, Paul responds to the question of whether a married couple should now live celibate lives. He is opposed to that. In marriage, the partners have agreed to share not only their worldly goods, their lives, but also their bodies. That is the nature of marriage. One partner cannot suddenly withdraw from that agreement. To all the philosophical ideas of marriage Paul adds the strong view from Judaism that prohibits sex outside of marriage. It is also interesting that Paul, who so often has been maligned as a misogynist, deals with the question of those who are already married in a very evenhanded way.[3] A married couple has some obligations to each other. One of them cannot simply decide to be celibate. Both must agree to this if it is to happen. Furthermore, Paul is somewhat skeptical that a married couple should make such a decision permanently—"for a set time" perhaps, and by mutual agreement, especially if the purpose is a season of prayer. But a sudden decision for a celibate life is dangerous for a married couple. It may well lead one or both of them into illicit situations. In this matter, the rights of a wife and those of a husband are the same. Each owes the other a certain intimacy that cannot suddenly be withdrawn because of their newfound faith.

A life of contented celibacy is a gift, a charism, of God. Paul is sure he has received this gift, and, under the circumstances, he wishes everyone had it. But he knows they do not. God's gifts are not uniform. Paul deals with the gift of celibacy in the same way that in 1 Corinthians 12–14 he deals with the question of speaking in tongues. They are both gifts of the Spirit, but not everyone has every gift. All gifts are to be used for the good of the whole body. Celibacy is like that. Those who have such a gift are to live in that manner and not assume they are superior to those who have other gifts. If the gift of celibacy is not present, the unmarried should marry.

Thus far, from 7:1-9, Paul's response to the Corinthians parallels much in the Greek and Roman literature. He does have a stronger emphasis on the equality of the relationship between husband and wife, although it is sometimes mentioned in the other literature. However, when we come to the latter part of the chapter, more specifically Christian reasons emerge.

In 7:26, Paul speaks of "the impending crisis," a phrase that can also be translated as "the present pressure." In other words, whether the Corinthians were currently in a crisis or the signs were there that one was about to begin, it is obvious that they are facing serious difficulties. It would be possible to assume this was a local situation, and it may well have been. However, in Paul's mind, whatever the situation was in Corinth, it bore a resemblance to the difficulties expected by Christians before the return of Christ at the end of history. In 7:29, Paul writes that "the appointed time has grown short." It is not simply a matter that Christ is about to return but that there will be great tribulation before his return.

Paul did expect the end of the world soon. In 7:31 he writes that "the present form of this world is passing away." If persecution and trials are to be the lot of Christians in the immediate future, then marrying and having children is not a very good idea. Parents have to be concerned about their children, and in a time of persecution their loyalties would naturally be divided. Their need to be faithful and therefore perhaps martyred would vie with their responsibility for their children. It would be best for those who are not yet married to remain single so that they could avoid any such difficult choices.

It is not that Paul is opposed to human sexuality. It is rather that he has very different priorities, priorities that make marriage and children quite secondary. He clearly supports celibacy as a preferable state to marriage, and that is something unheard of in Israel. We cannot assume that Paul had been influenced by ascetic notions in the surrounding Greek culture. His reasons for celibacy have nothing to do with asceticism. He assumes that this history as we know it is soon to end with the return of Christ. Before that, there may be terrible suffering. Therefore it would be better to use the little time remaining to be about the Lord's work rather than going on as usual.

In Matthew, the coming of Christ is likened to the days of Noah: "For as in those days before the flood they were eating and drinking, marrying and giving in marriage, until the day Noah entered the ark, and they knew nothing until the flood came and swept them all away, so too will be the coming of the Son of Man" (Matthew 24:38-39). Marrying and giving in marriage are synonymous with normal human life that expects the generations to continue. The same point is made in Luke's Gospel, in response to a question asked by some Sadducees about the resurrection life in the instance of a levirate marriage where seven brothers married the same woman. Jesus responds: "Those who belong to this age marry and are given in marriage; but those who are considered worthy of a place in that age and in the resurrection from the dead neither marry nor are given in marriage. Indeed they cannot die anymore, because they are like angels and are children of God, being children of the resurrection" (Luke 20:34-36).

For Paul, the faithful should realize that this present life is not going to go on as usual. The end is at hand. That should make a dramatic difference in how they lead their lives in the remaining time. Celibacy, for him, does not seem to be a value in itself, as though sex were something unclean. Rather, it is distracting to go on living as though nothing had changed when in reality everything is about to change dramatically. The advice he gives to widows is the same as to virgins: it would be better not to marry because then you will have more time and concern for the things that need to be done in this brief period before the end. Virgins are not somehow of a higher order than the widows. Both are simply presently unattached, and it would be well to remain that way.

At the same time, Paul is well aware that even great faith and awareness of the nearness of the end times may not be sufficient to overcome the power of sexual attraction. In that case, it would be better to marry than either to yield to the temptation of illicit sex or have one's mind always distracted by desire. Marriage is an honorable state, and the ability to be happily celibate is a gift of God. Paul is aware, however, that not everyone has been given that particular gift.

Furthermore, if the end of history is at hand, the question of providing future generations is moot. Paul is obviously not anticipating that there will be time for even the most favored believers to see their children's children, unless they are already on the scene. Celibacy is, for him, a very positive choice, given the reality of the times. His words parallel the passage in the Gospel of Matthew, after Jesus' words about divorce:

> His disciples said to him: "If such is the case of a man with his wife, it is better not to marry." But he said to them, "Not everyone can accept this teaching, but only those to whom it is given. For there are eunuchs who have been so from birth, and there are eunuchs who have been made eunuchs by others, and there are eunuchs who have made themselves eunuchs for the sake of the kingdom of heaven. Let anyone accept this who can." (Matthew 19:10-12)

If one assumes that voluntary celibacy is what is meant by those "who have made themselves eunuchs for the sake of the kingdom of heaven," then here is also the word that such celibacy is a gift that not everyone receives. It is a purposeful celibacy eschatologically oriented toward the kingdom, not simply a rejection of human sexuality as somehow evil.

What should we do with this passage today? After twenty centuries it is a little difficult to assume that marrying and giving in marriage should be put off because the end of this history is at hand.

Celibacy is not a topic that will find much sympathy, unless we stress it only for those not yet married. But this passage raises several questions for us. Is there any place in the church for a celibate life? Can Paul's words have any meaning for Christians in the twenty-first century? Given the character of our sex-saturated times, if someone were given "the gift of celibacy" he or she would probably go to a therapist to get rid of it. In 1967, Pope Paul VI, writing a defense of the requirement of priestly celibacy, listed all of the arguments against it. One of the objections (which he later in the paper refuted) stated what is probably the common view in our society. He wrote: "There are also some who strongly maintain that priests by reason of their celibacy find themselves in a situation that is physically and psychologically detrimental to the development of a mature and well-balanced human personality."[4] For many in our society, a life without sexual activity is immature. No wonder many early adolescents seek sexual initiation in order to prove that they have become adults. To call hard-core pornography "adult" is to confuse matters even more, as though "mature audiences" ought to appreciate it, and only the immature would find it offensive. Our culture finds celibacy strange, archaic, and an unhealthy choice for "normal" human beings precisely because of the assumption that normal human beings engage in sexual activity very frequently, whether married or unmarried.

For Protestants, there are added factors that must be taken into consideration. At the time of the Protestant Reformation in the sixteenth century, the Reformers took issue both with the idea that clergy must be celibate and with the view that monasticism was a legitimate vocation. At the heart of both concerns was the Protestant rejection of the idea that celibacy was a higher state than marriage. The reasons for this ranking throughout the Middle Ages was the belief that sex was a necessary evil for procreation, but sexual desire was the result of the Fall and therefore sinful. Sex within marriage was legitimate only because it led to procreation. This had been the teaching of Saint Augustine in the fourth and early fifth centuries, and it strongly influenced all of the Western church. Augustine had not invented such ideas, rather they had been a part of the acculturation of the church in the societies of the Roman Empire. The reasons for celibacy, therefore, were quite different from those given by Paul.

The Reformers totally opposed the idea that celibacy was superior to marriage. They lifted up not only the goal of procreation but also the significance of companionship. Not only could clergy marry, but the minister's family became a new witness to the meaning of the companionship for which we were all created. Monasteries and convents were closed in Protestant areas. All of this was quite positive for marriage. However, very few Protestant churches had any place for the unmarried. Some Anabaptists groups such as the Hutterites did have a place, as did the later Pietist group, the Moravians. In both cases, the whole congregation lived as a community, with houses for single men and single women, as well as for married couples. All groups were equally part of the community, with the larger context providing companionship.

The Reformers themselves did assume that some people might well remain unmarried, but what they opposed was a vow of celibacy required of anyone. As Paul says, celibacy is a gift of God. For the Reformers, to require a vow of lifelong celibacy would be to presume on the grace of God. Perhaps the gift of celibacy would be there for a lifetime, but then again perhaps it would be withdrawn after a few years. One should not assume that if one took such a vow God would supply the gift. Therefore one must always leave open the option of marriage.[5]

Many Protestant churches give the impression that marriage is the only normal and legitimate form of life for adults. "Singles" need a special ministry precisely because they do not fit into the expected pattern of congregational life. A Roman Catholic author, writing sketches of those she considered "saints," included John Wesley, the founder of Methodism, among them. Noting his dismal venture into love and marriage, she wrote: "If ever a saint was destined for the single life it was John. But as a good Protestant he fancied that celibacy bore a popish taint."[6]

There have been some exceptions to this Protestant dislike of celibacy. In the late-nineteenth and early-twentieth century, many Protestant churches developed boards for sending women missionaries. Married couples were sent by the general boards of mission, but these women's boards sent only single women and fully expected that they would remain single.[7] Orders of deaconesses also were developed for various missions within the society, such as teaching and nursing. These women also were expected to remain single in order to continue in their roles. No formal "vows of celibacy" were taken, but the expectation was very clear.

At the present time, the whole issue of homosexuality within the church again has raised the question of whether or not lifelong celibacy ought to be demanded or expected of a group within the church. Nor has the church considered the wider issue of what heterosexual people should do who have not received the gift of celibacy and yet have not found a suitable marriage partner. Perhaps it was easier in a time when marriages were at least in part arranged so that the task of finding a mate was not left to the individuals alone.

The question still must be asked and, at least to some degree, answered: What do we do with Paul's words about celibacy today? Was Paul mistaken that the end was about to come? Since he seemed to mean the end of this history as we know it, in a way that was obvious to everyone, of course he was mistaken. However, what he understood, and what the early church clearly believed, was the realization that in some strange way the end had come. At least the beginning of the end had come. It had come in the resurrection of Jesus on that first Easter. It was known and experienced only by the faithful, but the end had truly begun. At some point the end would fully come, and then with the return of Christ it would be visible and obvious to all. But now, in the meantime, the end has begun for the faithful, even though in a way hidden from those who are not in Christ.

Paul was mistaken about the time of the full manifestation of the end. We, however, and most of the church for many centuries have lost the other realization, that for us, the faithful, the end has truly begun. The resurrection of Jesus marked the inbreaking of the new age. Those who in baptism died and rose with him also began participating in this new age, this new creation. They had received the Holy Spirit as the foretaste or down payment or guarantee of this new life (2 Corinthians 5:5). In the Eucharist, on the Lord's Day, at the Lord's Table, they encounter the risen Lord in a foretaste of the heavenly banquet.

Shortly after Paul's time and until very recently, the church lost much of this sense that it lived at all in the end times. Increasingly, people believed that only after death would Christians begin eternal life. For now, they held, the old world continues; and they needed to do what was necessary to ensure that after death they would enter the kingdom of heaven. Therefore the words of Paul about the nearness of the end and how that should change our priorities fell on deaf ears.

Of course throughout the medieval period great stress was laid on a celibate life in the monastic vocation, but often this was seen as a means of gaining heaven or for other reasons, not as a response to already living in the end times. Baptism and Eucharist also lost the eschatological meaning they had held in the early church.

In the last fifty years there has been a resurgence of the understanding that Christians are to see themselves as having joined Christ in his death to the old life, and in some mysterious fashion they, even now, have begun to be raised with him to new life, the life of the new creation.

If we regain a sense that, for us, the end of this old world is indeed at hand, and in fact we have already begun to participate in the new world that is coming, what then would that do for our understanding of these words of Paul to the Corinthians?

First, in this old world of an overabundance of sexual stimulation on all sides, we need to recapture the truth that some may indeed receive the gift of celibacy, and help people be open to it. Not everyone is called to the vocation of marriage. This means recognizing and valuing those who lead such a life as exercising a grace that has been given to them for the sake of the whole church, just as other gifts are received for the whole church. Our common terms for never-married adults are generally pejorative, showing that we really do not believe that it is a legitimate way of life. It also means that those who are celibate need to see what contribution their state in life makes possible for the good of the mission of the whole church. Are they free to take on different responsibilities? How can the congregation support them with the community and friendships they need as human beings? Protestants have convinced themselves that marriage is as honorable a state as celibacy. Now we need to be clear that celibacy is as honorable a state as marriage.

Second, we need to recognize that the situation of modern young people makes the decision about sexual behavior much more difficult than it was in past ages. Young people are surrounded by sexual stimuli. Their adolescence has been greatly extended. That is to say, their physical maturity is present long before their social maturity. What are their choices? They are (1) to be sexually abstinent, which in such a sexually explicit culture is very difficult, especially if they do not have the gift of celibacy; (2) to marry, even though the partners may in the future develop in such radically different ways that divorce is likely; (3) to be involved in monogamous or serial sexual relationships without marriage, until the time seems right for total commitment; or (4) to be promiscuous.

A fifth choice might be possible if the partners had a common faith commitment within which they anticipated future growth. It would allow each of them the room to change, but within the parameters of their common faith. Then a relatively early marriage might work. Such faith commitment, however, is not common in adolescence. Young people may be sincere Christians and therefore assume that if two devout Christians marry, all the difficulties will be solved. The problem is that such young people often believe Christian faith is something static, something one must hold on to unaltered. It is hard for them to imagine that a deep Christian faith might lead one to change rather drastically from adolescence to maturity. One might change vocations, or even ideas about what constitutes success, or what is really moral in terms of foreign policy or the use of money or family relationships. How can two people be committed to each other in the context of a common Christian faith and still assume that they will both change? How can they be prepared to negotiate such change within the context of a committed marriage?

The church needs to be able to speak both to the choices and to the problems that young people face. There needs to be clear recognition of how the options have changed, or at least how the traditional options have become much more difficult. At the same time, the church needs to help both young people considering marriage and older people already married understand ways in which growth and change can occur positively within the context of a committed marriage.

Third, congregations need to have frank and intergenerational discussions about how to combat the effects of the current cultural situation. Sex is important in human life. It is the good gift of God. It is for companionship as well as procreation. However, it is not the central focus of the life of a Christian. Because the end has begun, Paul is right: our priorities have changed from those of the world around us. We are living now as those who have one foot in this world and one in the world to come, where there will be no marriage or giving in marriage. Marriage remains a good gift of God. Children are also a wonderful gift from God. But for Christians, things have changed. Our future is not simply our children and our children's children. Our future is the kingdom of God. Those who marry and those who do not; those who have children and those who do not—all have this same future toward which, and in which, they live their lives of faith as the one body of Christ.

Congregations that neatly divide into groups of singles, married couples with children, and so forth, perpetuate the patterns of the society around them. It would be far better for congregations to be a witness to the world of a healthy and inclusive community that makes no such distinctions, because all of the members have this common foothold in the future that has begun, a future in which "there will be no marriage or giving in marriage."

Preaching This Text Today

First, the preacher would do well to begin by acknowledging that this is a very strange passage and even list the reasons why it seems irrelevant to us. Second, it needs to be pointed out that though in almost every other case there is enormous continuity between the Old Testament and the New Testament, on the issue of celibacy there is a clear contrast. We are more comfortable with Israel's view than with the early church's. It would also be necessary to distinguish Paul's view from that of the medieval period, to prepare people for something other than what they probably think the passage is saying. All of this could be done fairly quickly as an introduction.

The sermon proper could then show why this text does teach us something significant about the gospel and about our lives as Christians. This could point to the life of the congregation as a whole more than to individual lives. Questions could be raised about how needed discussions about sexuality could be held, or how single and married people could be more integrated into the life of the congregation. So often sermons are directed to each individual's life but not to the corporate life of the congregation. This text could deal with the congregation quite directly. The sermon could raise a variety of issues that later could be dealt with by various programmatic committees in the congregation. It would be very interesting to preach this at a point when the congregation is considering beginning a singles' ministry.

Above all, this passage could help a congregation see the significance of understanding themselves as already participating in the life of the new creation. This is true in all of our lives, not just what we think of as religious. Our family lives, our sex lives, our relationship to those Christians whose lives are quite different from ours—all of this is changed from the surrounding society because in Christ all things have been transformed. If there were communion following the sermon, then the eschatological focus could be experienced in a new way. That would mean that this passage, while focusing on human sexuality, is really focused on what it means to be living in the "already but not yet" character of the Christian life.

SUGGESTED READING

Deming, Will. *Paul on Marriage and Celibacy: The Hellenistic Background of 1 Corinthians 7.* Cambridge: Cambridge University Press, 1995.

Orr, William F. and James Arthur Walther. *1 Corinthians: A New Translation.* Anchor Bible. Garden City, N.Y.: Doubleday, 1976.

Robinson, Archibald and Alfred Plummer. *A Critical and Exegetical Commentary on the First Epistle of St. Paul to the Corinthians.*

International Critical Commentary. Edinburgh: T. & T. Clark, 2nd ed., 1914.

Sampley, J. Paul. "The First Letter of Paul to the Corinthians," in *The New Interpreter's Bible*, vol. 10. Nashville: Abingdon Press, 2002.

Yarbrough, Larry O. *Not Like the Gentiles: Marriage Rules in the Letters of Paul*. SBL Dissertation Series 80. Atlanta: Scholars Press, 1986.

CHAPTER THREE

Blest Handkerchiefs and Demons

THE TEXT

Acts 19:11-20

> God did extraordinary miracles through Paul, so that when the
> handkerchiefs or aprons that had touched his skin were brought
> to the sick, their diseases left them, and the evil spirits came out
> of them. Then some itinerant Jewish exorcists tried to use the
> name of the Lord Jesus over those who had evil spirits, saying,
> "I adjure you by the Jesus whom Paul proclaims." Seven sons of
> a Jewish high priest named Sceva were doing this. But the evil
> spirit said to them in reply, "Jesus I know, and Paul I know; but
> who are you?" Then the man with the evil spirit leaped on
> them, mastered them all, and so overpowered them that they
> fled out of the house naked and wounded. When this became
> known to all residents of Ephesus, both Jews and Greeks, every-
> one was awestruck; and the name of the Lord Jesus was praised.
> Also many of those who became believers confessed and dis-
> closed their practices. A number of those who practiced magic
> collected their books and burned them publicly; when the value
> of these books was calculated, it was found to come to fifty
> thousand silver coins. So the word of the Lord grew mightily
> and prevailed.

THE DIFFICULTY

There is a great deal of the Bible that at first glace is very strange, such as this text from Acts, and many preachers quickly move on to parts that make more sense. However, if we were to eliminate from our "preachable Bible" all the passages that deal with strange ideas and customs, we would have a small Bible indeed.

The biblical material we now possess was produced over a period of hundreds of years and in a variety of cultural settings, from semi-nomadic tribes to the cosmopolitan Roman Empire. The social structures of each of these settings have left their marks on the writings. The word of God always comes to people in the midst of a particular culture. There is no culture-free revelation. Nor is it easy for God's people in later centuries to distinguish what is truly revelation for them as well as for the ancient people, from what is the cultural material that is no longer relevant. There is no reason to assume that in the twenty-first century we should try to re-create life in tribal Israel or the social structures of the first century Roman Empire.

At least two significant problems emerge from the contrast between the worldviews and common social assumptions found in Scripture, and those held in our society today. First, what are we to do with the strange events we find in Scripture that are unbeliev-able in our society? This includes both what are generally termed miracles as well as the demonic activity that appears so frequently, particularly in the New Testament. Second, what are we to do with the social assumptions and expectations that were part of earlier societies but are not part of ours?

On the first issue, the passages about miracles and demons come into conflict with the way in which our culture determines truth. We live in a time when truth is measured in scientific terms. What is believable is that which conforms to certain expectations that have general acceptance by educated people. These things can be proved through objective, repeatable, experimental means. This includes the beginning of our world eons ago and its evolution over that span of time.

In the ancient world there was room for mystery. There was the expectation that powers of good and evil beyond the human level are active in our world. Even in the case of diseases, physical and mental, powers and causes beyond the human ability to know were seen at work. People then, as now, demanded to know what caused various ills. They found the causes in forces beyond the human level. Now we have learned a great deal about such matters. We have discovered causes that people in ancient times knew nothing about: viruses, bacteria, genetic defects, and so forth. What do we do, then, with biblical passages that make no sense to a modern mind? Our tendency is to ignore them.

However, a science-dominated culture that does not like mystery, that seeks not only to understand everything but also to control it, is, for many contemporaries, quite sterile. It is no surprise, then, that many people are seeking a way to regain some sense of the mystery that surrounds us. Many of the New Age ideas that are rampant in our society are attractive precisely because they attempt to tap into a sense of mystery, of being surrounded by forces beyond the human being. Whether it is a *Star Wars* blessing of "May the Force be with you," or concepts drawn from ancient religions, there is some desire for a greater sense of mystery surrounding human life.[1]

In the midst of this conflict between a modern scientific worldview and the biblical material, churches have been divided over how to respond. Some churches call upon their members to hold the same worldview as the ancients held. This is a minority opinion, but strong in some fundamentalist circles. Some churches expect their members to hold as true everything stated in Scripture, but then to live in today's world with a contemporary viewpoint. In other words, miracles and demonic activity are to be accepted as happening back then, but they are not expected in today's world. Live now in a scientifically defined world, but believe that in the world of the Bible things happened as they are reported. Still, other churches try to explain those ancient happenings in terms that make sense scientifically today: demon possession readily becomes mental illness or epilepsy, depending on the description of symptoms; rising from the dead becomes leaving a catatonic state, and so forth.

None of these options is particularly satisfying. Most of us simply try to ignore those passages that are the most peculiar, and spend our energy trying to deal with the central issues of God's presence in Jesus Christ, and God's work in the midst of our world.

Yet such a procedure removes much of the Scripture from our reach. It leaves us with a truncated witness to God's revelation. Either those strange passages contain nothing that could be God's word to us, and so we can rightly ignore it, or else God's revelation to us as well as to those ancient people is somehow in the midst of these peculiar passages, and we need to be open to it.

The second issue concerns the discrepancy between our contemporary social structures and that of the ancient world. However, there is no single, normative social structure in the Bible. There is enormous difference between the life of the Hebrew people in the time of the patriarchs, living in tents, with polygamy as an acceptable form; the time of tribal organization in the days of the judges; the settled, urban life of the Davidic monarchy; and the time of Jesus and the New Testament church in the midst of the Roman Empire.

For instance, there is ambivalence in churches about Old Testament laws. Many Christian traditions distinguish between what they term the ceremonial law and the moral law of Israel, and hold that the ceremonial law is not a law for Christians. Often the "Council of Jerusalem" mentioned in Acts 15 is the basis for this understanding. The letter sent to Gentile converts reads: "[I]t has seemed good to the Holy Spirit and to us to impose on you no further burden than these essentials: that you abstain from what has been sacrificed to idols and from blood and from what is strangled and from fornication. If you keep yourselves from these, you will do well" (Acts 15:28-29). That would seem to take care of the food laws and laws of sexual purity to be found in the Pentateuch, among other things. However, it is obviously not that simple. Paul himself dealt differently with the question of food sacrificed to idols (1 Corinthians 8), and most Christians today have no religious scruples against eating blood sausages. Some Christian traditions have applied the Sabbath laws to their own members. The laws about usury (Deuteronomy 23:19-20) were upheld in the Middle Ages.

Obviously, the line between ceremonial and moral law is not easy to determine. We need to see if there is a word from God to us even in strange legislation from an ancient world. We cannot automatically ignore passages from the Bible that deal with an alien social setting. In fact, the history of the church's dealing with the

Sabbath laws is instructive in this regard. Some churches ignore those laws completely, assuming that they were ceremonial laws for Israel and therefore with no meaning for Christians. A few groups completely disagree with this, and hold that Christians are under these laws, including holding their worship services on Saturday, the seventh day. Some groups, notably the Puritans, assumed that Christians were governed by these laws, but on the first day of the week rather than on the last. Legislation in the United States that prohibited stores and theaters from being open on Sunday, or prohibited Sunday sports events, stem from this understanding. In some communities in the New England colonies, cooking was not done on Sunday. All of this is generally referred to as "Sabbatarianism," taking the Old Testament legislation about the Sabbath and applying it to the Christian Sunday.

In more recent years, Sabbatarianism has lessened considerably, and the power of churches to maintain the legal status of such laws has eroded completely. The wider society assumes that Sunday can be like any other day as far as shopping and leisure activities are concerned. Even in the churches, there is less and less tendency to apply these laws to Christians' private lives. In fact, the pendulum has swung so far in the other direction that parents now often have to choose whether their children will go to church and Sunday school on Sunday morning or play on a soccer team.

At the same time that this change toward secularism is taking place in our society, there is another phenomenon occurring. Many Christians are taking a new look at the ancient Sabbath legislation and saying there is a word from God to us to be found in it, and indeed, a word we very much need to hear. The reasons for recapturing the Sabbath are not legalistic, but rather come from seeing what the celebration of the Sabbath has done in Jewish life. On this basis, several reasons for recapturing the Sabbath can be given: it helps maintain the sense of identity because it is the whole religious community that keeps Sabbath and therefore our keeping it distinguishes us from secular neighbors; it provides a respite from our contemporary frenetic lifestyle, and allows us to become centered on ultimate values; it reminds us that we are creatures and therefore need frequent times of rest and renewal; it gives us the opportunity to prepare ourselves for corporate worship on Sunday (this is particularly true if the Sabbath is understood to begin on

Saturday night). All of these values can involve the whole family and can strengthen its ties as family and as part of the wider community of faith. It is not Sabbatarian, but it is also not a disregard of biblical material that on the face of it could be viewed as irrelevant. The same kind of exercise may be done with much of the ancient material that is usually judged useless for Christian preaching.

Often these two issues—the conflict between modern, scientific understandings and miracles, and the conflict between ancient social patterns and a modern democratic society—are treated separately. Obviously, both are worthy of discussion. However, it is important to see that they both stem from a common source: the conflict between our contemporary social understandings and the prescientific, premodern world in which Scripture was formed. In addition, there is, as we shall see, a common theological and biblical rationale for looking at these two conflicts together.

OTHER BIBLICAL VOICES

Because ancient cultures present us with these two problems when we look at ancient texts—problems with different worldviews, and problems with different social structures—we shall look first at some passages that help provide a theological understanding of both sorts of difficulties. We shall then look at a passage that concerns ancient social structures and then, in greater depth, return to the selected text for a sermon.

(1) Genesis 3:8–4:16

In a fallen creation thorns and thistles, and pain and murder occur. The faith of Israel and of the early church was that the world God created was good, but because of sin the creation had fallen from that totally good state. Therefore one cannot simply say that the world we live in is as God created it, and good. However, we understand the fall story today; it means that disease, birth defects, natural disasters (such as floods and earthquakes), disrupted human relationships, and even death itself are all part of the fallenness of creation. In the new creation these things will not occur.

Many passages in the New Testament present Jesus as the one who is able to overcome the fallenness of creation itself. The healing miracles of Jesus were not simply incidents of curing, the way a doctor might accomplish it today. Nor are they any reason to assume that faith will heal all things and we should not use modern medicine. The healings in the New Testament are signs of the inbreaking of the new creation that is happening precisely because the Messiah has come. It is a new creation, but it is also a restoration of much that was lost in the fall of the old creation. Therefore when Jesus heals someone or calms a storm at sea, he is not simply dealing with a particular person's problem. Rather, his action is a sign, a foretaste, a sample, of that new age that is only beginning to break into this old world, an inbreaking now known only to faith. These events point to his role as Messiah. This is particularly to be seen in the words of Jesus concerning the man who was born blind. Jesus was asked who was responsible for the man's blindness. He replied: "Neither this man nor his parents sinned; he was born blind so that God's works might be revealed in him. We must work the works of him who sent me while it is day; night is coming when no one can work. As long as I am in the world, I am the light of the world" (John 9:3-5). The signs of who Jesus really was were there for the time being, indicating the inbreaking of the new age.

It is not only physical ailments that have been caused by the fall. Human relationships have also been damaged by it. The man and woman blame each other, and brothers kill each other. It is the character of the world we live in. It is against this background that we can see the radical nature of the love that Christians are to display. Love for those who are enemies; love for those who are in no position to do anything for us; love for those who disagree with us; love for family and friends who are difficult; love for all of these is a miracle. It is as much a miracle as the sudden and unexpected healing of a sick person. It is the healing of a sick relationship.

Many who read this do not believe that there are demons as such operating in our world. However, in eliminating demons we may also have eliminated the sense that this world is, at least to some degree, under the power of evil. God created a good world, but something has happened to that original creation. In fact, the Bible deals even more comprehensively with the effects of evil than we usually imagine. It assumes that before the fall, animals and humans lived easily with one another, not fearfully. Afterward, animals ate each other, humans ate animals, and fearfulness entered in (see Genesis 1:29-31; 9:2-3). Part of the vision of the redemption of the world includes what has been termed "the peaceable kingdom." Animals in our old world that are afraid of one another—with good reason—will be at peace. "The wolf shall live with the lamb.... The cow and the bear shall graze, their young shall lie down together; and the lion shall eat straw like the ox" (Isaiah 11:6, 7). Even a human child will be safe in this environment of wild animals. It is no accident that paintings of "the peaceable kingdom" often appear on Christmas cards. The passage in Isaiah assumes that this peace in creation will be inaugurated by the righteous king from the tribe of Jesse, who Christians believe is Jesus.

We must not lose that sense of the reality and power of evil in our world, for it is central to the whole Bible. We may picture it differently than people did in the first century, but to understand the work of Christ, the meaning of the cross and resurrection, the dawn of the reign of God in our midst, and our own call to discipleship, we need to understand the power of evil that Christ has conquered. We do not see that victory in its fullness. In fact, it is known only to faith. Our call to discipleship is, however, the call to live out of that reality—that evil has lost its ultimate power—and not out of the reality that we see in our old world, where evil still holds sway. For most Christians, miraculous changes in human relationships as a result of love may be the most visible sign of this victory of Christ and the inbreaking of the new creation. On other occasions, it may be surprising health where only sickness was expected. The new creation is breaking into this old world. That is the message of Easter. The faithful are witnesses to and vehicles of this victory. With this perspective in mind, an approach to passages that deal with miracles and those that deal with changes in human relationships and social structures can be similar.

(2) Colossians 3:18–4:1

Three times in the New Testament we find counsel given to various human relationships: wives and husbands, children and fathers, slaves and masters. These are to be found in different forms in Ephesians 5:21–6:9; 1 Peter 2:18–3:7 (which does not include anything about children); and Colossians 3:18–4:1. It is this last one that we will look at.

Today in our culture the particular verses of this passage of interest are those concerning wives. These are indeed difficult and challenging verses. Wives are told to be subject to their husbands. The reason these verses are now so controversial is because they deal with an issue that is of great relevance, given the contemporary women's movement.

Two centuries ago, the verses about wives probably would have caused little comment, precisely because these verses agreed with the common wisdom of the day. In the early-nineteenth century, few people were raising questions about the role of wives. The section on slaves, however, was of considerable difficulty in the decades before the U.S. Civil War. In verse 22, slaves are told to obey their earthly masters. Those who favored slavery could use these verses to show that the Bible supported the institution of slavery, or at least had no objection to it. Those who were opposed to slavery found the passage challenging. Part of the battle at the time was the issue of holding to Scripture or discounting the passages that were found unacceptable. Needless to say, it was the supporters of slavery that seemed to hold firm to biblical teaching, and it was the abolitionists who were considered to be playing fast and loose with the written word of God.

How are we to deal with these verses about slavery today? We are in a different situation because the institution of slavery itself is no longer a part of our society, and no one is eager to reinstate it. Are these verses, then, of no concern to us because we have no slaves? Have they lost their character as the word of God? Were the slaveholders right in saying that the Bible supported slavery?

On the same grounds, is it true that the Bible supports the subjection of wives today? Where the lectionary includes any part of the household legislation, it eliminates the words about slavery, probably because they do seem irrelevant. However, keeping that section as part of the pericope helps us interpret the whole passage, because we are faced with the question of why one part is irrelevant and can be discounted whereas another section is seen as appropriate for today. It makes us ask, What can be attributed to the culture of the time, and what is a matter of revelation that is relevant for us and all Christians at all times?

If we do not take words about wives or slaves out of the context of the whole passage, they can be seen in another light. It is not only the weaker part of the pair that is spoken about in each case. Husbands are told to love their wives and not treat them harshly. Masters are reminded that they too have a master in heaven, and they are to treat their slaves justly. All of this is in the context of the new life that has been gained for all who are in Christ. They have already been reminded that, since they have been clothed in a new life, the distinctions between slave and free, between Greek and Jew, and so forth, no longer hold. They are all alike. They are God's chosen (Colossians 3:9-15). The mark of this new life is love, expressed in forgiveness. It is in this context that the weaker of the pairs—wives and slaves—are told to be subject. It is in this context also that husbands and masters are told to be gentle and fair. All of this is contrary to what would be expected of husbands and masters in Roman society of the time. Furthermore, the wives who are being addressed are most likely not married to the husbands who are hearing the words. In other words, the early church had as members many wives whose husbands were not members, as well as many slaves whose masters were not Christians. Within the congregation, however, they were to treat each other as equal, as new creatures: "If anyone has a complaint against another, forgive each other; just as the Lord has forgiven you, so you also must forgive. Above all, clothe yourselves with love" (Colossians 3:13*b*-14*a*).

The bottom line is that love is to be the hallmark of all Christians in all circumstances. Being oppressed is not an excuse for not loving. It is an opportunity for forgiving. At the same time, those who have power are called to love and to be just. Christians in the first century were in no position to alter the social institutions of marriage and slavery. Even Christian husbands and masters were severely limited by law in terms of their powers to change the institutions of marriage and slavery. The concern of slaves and masters, husbands and wives was how to live out the new life of love in the midst of the institutions they had inherited. Granted, if both the husband and wife or both the slave and master were Christians, there might be new possibilities in terms of their private relationship. This is the word of Paul in his letter to Philemon in which Philemon, the master, was asked by Paul to love the returned runaway slave "no longer as a slave but more than a slave, a beloved brother" (Philemon 16). The public institution, however, was beyond their power to change.[2]

We have not touched on the issue of children. They are told to obey their parents. The parents who are addressed, however, are fathers, that is, male parents and not parents in general (Colossians 3:21). That is because the power of the father in that society was far greater than the power of the mother. Fathers are told not to provoke their children. Again, love is the rule in all relationships. In our day it is possible for the mother to be as abusive as the father. Power relationships have changed, especially as we have moved from the Roman household that included the whole extended family to our nuclear family that gives much more power to both parents in the privacy of their home.

What are we to do with this household legislation today? We live in a very different setting. We take for granted that slavery should not exist. The legal situation of wives has also changed. There are laws against the abuse of wives and children that would not have been imaginable in ancient Rome. Can we say that a major reason the situation has changed is because these passages were taken seriously? Yes, to some degree we can. The church eventually affected the whole society of the Roman Empire and its descendants to the extent that institutions actually changed. Granted, it took a very long time, and the changes are not complete. We cannot, however, overlook the transformations that have taken place, and ignore the role the teachings of the church had in this matter.

What, then, does this passage about slaves, wives, and children mean for us in our society today? Our options in employment are very different from those of the ancient Roman Empire. We are not put into employment without our consent, nor do we need to stay in an intolerable situation. We can change employment. We can leave an abusive marriage. Children do not have to remain with an abusive parent. Such changes over the centuries are in part due to the message of the gospel. The requirements of fairness and justice have been institutionalized. It does not always work, but the ideal is there.

Freedom of choice however, is a relative matter. Many people are caught in jobs they do not want, and there are few alternatives for them. They may be in a difficult work relationship, and yet if they leave, they are without any resources. A woman may find herself in an abusive marriage; yet, without skills and with small children, she needs to weigh her options very carefully lest she find herself and her children in even harder circumstances. In both cases, if the situation were worse, the advice to leave it would be clear. But degrees of abusiveness exist, and options are not always so obvious.

There are other relationships we all find ourselves in: roommates in college, members of committees, neighbors with whom we must associate every day. Whether we leave the situation because it is intolerable or we stay because it is the better option, Christians continue to be told that they are to be loving and forgiving. This passage from Colossians provides a model of how Christians are to live out their lives. We are not told to put up with whatever injustice we find (although if the author believed the end of history was expected very soon, it could be assumed the person might as well stay in the situation). The author is saying that love is still the mark of the Christian. Such love and forgiveness are not human possibilities. They are the work of Christ in our lives; they are the unexpected responses made possible by Christ. Just as the words of Jesus in the Sermon on the Mount call us to love our enemies, the household legislation speaks of specific relationships in which an enemy might be identified. Love is required even here. It was required in the first century, even in the midst of slavery and oppressive marriages. It is still required today, even when we can leave abusive relationships. That is not an easy word to hear. We need to remember that it was no easier to hear when the letter was first written. Whenever such love occurs, it is more than a human possibility; it is a miracle. It is the inbreaking, in a partial but real way, of the new creation. It is also a healing of the old.

BACK TO THE TEXT: ACTS 19:11-20

This passage has a variety of things that most contemporary preachers would like to avoid: blest handkerchiefs and aprons that healed people; unsuccessful exorcists; talking demons; and book burnings. The passage occurs as part of a summary of Paul's work in the Roman province of Asia, which included Ephesus, a mission that lasted about two years. We are told that Paul's work included healing the sick, which continued the kind of work Jesus had carried out. Not only ordinary illnesses were healed, but also cases of demonic possession. Nor were these strange things happening only when Paul himself touched the sick people. It was enough that handkerchiefs or aprons touched Paul. These items then could heal the sick.

The author of Acts is clearly telling us that the same sort of sign of the inbreaking kingdom that was present in Jesus was also present in the ministry of Paul among the Gentiles. We should not be sidetracked by debates about the handkerchiefs and demons. Something astonishing was happening; people were being healed, and in some way the power of evil, in whose grasp this fallen creation has been held, was losing sway because of Paul's proclamation of the gospel. (Luke mentions the same sort of effect when the seventy returned from preaching. Jesus remarks, "I watched Satan fall from heaven like a flash of lightning" [Luke 10:18].) However we understand it, the setting of this narrative is the overcoming of some of the results of the fall of creation, the lessening of the powers of evil, because of Paul's proclamation of the gospel. They follow the pattern of Jesus himself.

Paul evidently had become quite famous with all of these healings, and others decided they would like to use this power. We are told that seven brothers, non-Christian Jews who were exorcists, tried using the name of Jesus to perform exorcisms. They did not believe in Jesus but called on his name indirectly, trying to defeat the powers of evil by calling on "the Jesus whom Paul proclaims." The results were disastrous for them. The demons, the powers of evil, knew that these exorcists lacked the power that Paul had. Instead of defeating the powers of evil, these exorcists were overpowered by evil.

What the evil spirit said to the exorcists was: "Jesus I know, and Paul I know; but who are you?" (Acts 19:15).[3] Two different verbs are used here for "I know." In the case of Jesus, the verb *ginosko* is used, indicating Jesus' direct authority. In the case of Paul, the verb *epistamai* is used, showing that Paul's authority has been experienced. Both Jesus and Paul are known to have authority over evil. The exorcists, however, have no such authority.[4] If we were to put this event in more contemporary language, we might say the following: Christians are empowered by the Holy Spirit to be witnesses to the new age begun in the life, death, and resurrection of Jesus Christ. When this is done authentically, the powers of evil in this world will be in opposition. Even if we are faithful witnesses, we cannot guarantee that evil will be overthrown instantly and publicly. Paul himself had enough instances in which he was unsuccessful in changing situations. The cross itself is a witness that conquering evil is not an easy or immediate victory. However, we can be sure that the demonic powers will come to know us even as they know Jesus and Paul, and we will have authority, even if it is not seen at the time. Those unfortunate exorcists tried to claim the power of Christ without themselves being faithful disciples. It will not work. In fact, judging from their situation, it can only make matters worse for those who try it.

Imagine a group of Christians trying to overcome some manifestation of evil power in their community. Drug dealing to the young people might be an example. If such Christians attempted to eradicate this evil simply by claiming the name of Jesus, that would hardly make a dent. In fact, the dealers might well turn on them, inflicting bodily harm or instilling fear in them. The name of Jesus is not a magical formula to be thrown at evil from a safe distance. If serious Christians were willing to follow Christ faithfully, unafraid of the danger, the powers of evil might well have to acknowledge them. Evil cannot be fought from a safe distance. The demonic forces knew Jesus, and they knew Paul. They did not know these exorcists who tried to stay at arm's length and throw the name of Jesus at evil without actually engaging themselves in the required discipleship.

It is not only those ancient exorcists who try to combat evil without putting themselves in any danger. We as Christians try it often ourselves. We may take pride in the fact that the powers of evil, whatever their manifestations in our world, do not know us. But were we truly witnesses to the inbreaking of the kingdom, those powers would know us well. If we Christians feel powerless against the forces that oppose the ways of God's reign, then the cure is more faithful discipleship, not distancing ourselves from the evil in the world.

There are examples throughout the history of the church in which the faithful witness of one person who would not shy away from confronting evil risked all and gained an astonishing public victory. There are also examples throughout that history of the faithful witness of a person who, boldly confronting evil, was martyred. Both are victories over evil. The Letter to the Hebrews points to this strange equality of witnesses:

And what more should I say? For time would fail me to tell of Gideon, Barak, Samson, Jephthah, of David and Samuel and the prophets—who through faith conquered kingdoms, administered justice, obtained promises, shut the mouths of lions, quenched raging fire, escaped the edge of the sword....Others suffered mocking and flogging, and even chains and imprisonment. They were stoned to death, they were sawn in two, they were killed by the sword. (Hebrews 11:32-34, 36-37a)

The immediate result may differ enormously: they may have a great, obvious victory or they may appear to be completely defeated. The reality, however, is the same. They have been faithful disciples. It is precisely that possibility of public defeat that makes confronting evil a risky business. Only when the person confronting it has the goal of being a faithful disciple, not being the public victor, can they dare to take such a risk.

The narrative about the unhappy exorcists continues. Evidently the story becomes known, and many are frightened at the power of this Jesus whom Paul preaches. It is also evident that this name of Jesus cannot be used lightly without serious consequences. The church grew, but the new believers realized they needed to get rid of their earlier ways of dealing with evil—that is, with what are termed their practices of magic. The city of Ephesus was well known for its production and use of books on magic.[5] That is what the unsuccessful exorcists had practiced: using a formula that somehow is supposed to have power in the words themselves. If you know the magic words, you can combat evil. They had used the name of "Jesus whom Paul preaches" in this way. Having seen what happened to them, believers decided they had better be rid of the books that contained such magical spells. So they brought out their books and burned them publicly. They decided, in light of what they had seen and heard, that they had better not try combining their practices of magic with their new-found faith in Christ.

Christians today may not have books of magic spells, but we have our own ways of dealing with evil. Most of the time we are pragmatic. Pragmatism is part of a modern scientific worldview. We decide what action can be taken on the basis of what will work. Working means overcoming the evil, eliminating it in an observable way. If we cannot be relatively sure the evil will be eliminated then there is no point spending our time and energy attacking it. As we saw in the Hebrews passage, that is hardly the approach that leads to possible martyrdom. Our temptation is to combine pragmatism with discipleship; and if they conflict, then the fact that something is "not going to work" becomes reason enough to abandon discipleship or assume that its demands do not make sense in our world. We forget that they did not make sense in the first century, either. They make sense only to faith. It is also true that abandoning the battle against evil essentially means that we have allowed evil to conquer us. There is no neutral role.

Although there are enormous cultural differences between the first-century Roman Empire and our contemporary society, we have several things in common. First, there is evil in our world that manifests itself in various ways. Second, Christ has conquered the powers of evil and calls his followers to live on the basis of the truth of that victory. Third, there is a counter worldview in the society around us that has a different way of dealing with evil, and we are tempted to follow that way instead of the way of faith. In Paul's day, the alien view was magic formulas. In our day, it is pragmatism. Fourth, we may try to combine our discipleship with this alien method, and that can lead to our being conquered by evil rather than conquering it.

If we avoid all the biblical passages that speak of demons and miracles as impossible to preach in today's world, we will have eliminated much of the significance of the gospel for our time. It is the triumph of pragmatism over the preaching of the gospel.

PREACHING THIS TEXT TODAY

In any passage that includes such odd items as demons, it behooves the preacher to prepare the congregation for the reading. At least, in the sermon, the preacher should acknowledge at the beginning that most of us approach such passages with skepticism or with some confusion. In fact, the preacher might well begin by speaking about such passages in general, and how the word of God to us is not only to be found in texts that are readily understandable because they do not seem foreign to our culture.

Something also needs to be said about the miracle stories about Jesus himself—that they are not simply unusual events but signs of the inbreaking of God's reign, and therefore marks of his messiahship. In Acts, Paul is continuing in this pattern, made possible by the dawning of the kingdom of God in the resurrection. The preacher might also stress that since the world we live in continues to have evil as a reality, we have something to learn from this strange passage about how to go about our own confrontations with evil.

With such a beginning, the congregation may then be ready to look at the text itself. The stress is on the words of the demon who acknowledges the power of Jesus and Paul, and questions the power of the exorcists. The issue is the authority of Christians in the face of the evil—the demonic powers—in this world. We are given authority, though it does not guarantee visible or immediate success. Two points in particular need to be made. First, Christians are not to keep themselves aloof from the world as though they should avoid evil at all costs in order to stay pure. They are called upon to engage evil because they know that in Christ the victory over it is assured, no matter how strong evil appears to us now. Second, only those who are truly disciples of Christ have this authority. We cannot stand on the sidelines and throw the name of Jesus at evil. We must be followers who know by faith that Christ has conquered evil, and act accordingly.

A final point comes from the concluding verses. Evidently, many in Ephesus who were part of the church had tried to hold on to their magic books as well as hold to their Christian faith. Many of us do the same thing with the wisdom of our society, which we try to combine with faith. When such halfhearted believers saw the true power that was at work in Paul, and the consequences of trying to keep the old ways while calling on the name of Jesus, they came forward and destroyed their books. Many of us go on in our Christian lives never fully committing ourselves. We miss the full power of the gospel that goes with real discipleship. It does not guarantee victories that the world can readily recognize, but such faith brings with it its own victories that show we are beginning to experience here and now the life of the world to come.

Luther's great hymn "A Mighty Fortress" emphasizes many of the same themes, and could be used after the sermon.

SUGGESTED READING

González, Justo L. *The Gospel of the Spirit*. Maryknoll, New York: Orbis Books, 2001.

Martin, Ralph P. *Ephesians, Colossians, and Philemon*. Interpretation: A Bible Commentary for Teaching and Preaching. Atlanta: John Knox, 1991.

Wall, Robert W. "The Acts of the Apostles," in *The New Interpreter's Bible*, vol. 10. Nashville: Abingdon Press, 2002.

CHAPTER FOUR

Shouldn't We Try to Get Ahead?

THE TEXT

Matthew 20:17-28

> While Jesus was going up to Jerusalem, he took the twelve disciples aside by themselves, and said to them on the way, "See, we are going up to Jerusalem, and the Son of Man will be handed over to the chief priests and scribes, and they will condemn him to death; then they will hand him over to the Gentiles to be mocked and flogged and crucified; and on the third day he will be raised."
>
> Then the mother of the sons of Zebedee came to him with her sons, and kneeling before him, she asked a favor of him. And he said to her, "What do you want?" She said to him, "Declare that these two sons of mine will sit, one at your right hand and one at your left, in your kingdom." But Jesus answered, "You do not know what you are asking. Are you able to drink the cup that I am about to drink?" They said to him, "We are able." He said to them, "You will indeed drink my cup, but to sit at my right hand and at my left, this is not mine to grant, but it is for those for whom it has been prepared by my father."
>
> When the ten heard it, they were angry with the two brothers. But Jesus called them to him and said, "You know that the rulers of the Gentiles lord it over them, and their great ones are tyrants over them. It will not be so among you; but whoever

wishes to be great among you must be your servant, and whoever wishes to be first among you must be your slave; just as the
Son of Man came not to be served but to serve, and to give his
life a ransom for many."

THE DIFFICULTY

People in every society seek security for themselves and their
families. In ours, security is usually based on economic or social
success. Unlike traditional ancient societies, for us status is not
directly related to family, to inherited wealth and title, though there
is more of that than most of us would like to acknowledge. For us
status is more in terms of our own role in society—our political,
social, and economic power. The "self-made man" is admired,
especially if there were clearly humble beginnings.

Granted, there are many things in our society that severely limit
the status we may seek. Race or ethnicity, gender, family income,
educational opportunities—all will have an effect. In fact, some
people may feel that there is no point at all in seeking or imagining
a different status because it is really beyond their reach. But even
within the most marginal groups, there are marks of status. Money
will usually be a major factor. The corner drug dealer is seeking status. So is the woman who hopes to "marry well," or the unwed
teenager who assumes that having a child will give her status. We
can value goals as to their social usefulness or social harm; we can
classify ethical and unethical means of attaining these goals. Most
of the time we are aware of the dynamics of status-seeking at work
around and even within us.

Status—publicly recognized significance, no matter how small
or local that public is—is the hallmark of success in our society.
There are acknowledged routes to success: education, networking,
mentoring, a proper career path. Whether it is the ministry, stock-
broking, or football, we assume pragmatic means to achieve our
goals. Today there may be little difference between Christians and
non-Christians in such thinking. There may even be little difference
between the career planning of people in the ministry and their
contemporaries in secular business or industry. The Christian, one
hopes, will stress that there must be only legitimate, ethical means

of attaining the goals, but the marks of success still may be similar to those of people who are not Christians.

Into this cultural mind-set comes the word of the gospel. Truly it goes in the opposite direction, telling us to shun status. It appears totally opposed to our usual marks of success. It fails any normal tests for pragmatism. Verses such as Matthew 6:19 ("Do not store up for yourselves treasures on earth"), or Matthew 20:26 ("Whoever wishes to be great among you must be your servant"), or Luke 9:23 ("If any want to become my followers, let them deny themselves and take up their cross daily and follow me") do not sound like the way to the kind of success valued in our society. In fact, in secular terms they sound more like advice on how to be a loser.

There are currently Christian groups that try to combine worldly status and wealth with the gospel itself. They proclaim a "gospel of success" or "a gospel of wealth." They assume that by following principles in Scripture one can become wealthy and successful in terms that our society will understand. That, however, is the crassest form of acculturation of the gospel. Denying ourselves is not a covert way to become financially successful. God does not promise that those who deny themselves will be rewarded in this life, at least rewarded in any way that secular society would recognize. Perhaps the conversation with God attributed to Saint Teresa is more to the point, that the way God treated friends was why God had so few.[1]

Probably most of us do not believe the extremes of the "gospel of success." But most of us probably do agree with some of its understandings, at least enough so that we can combine our faith with our daily lives lived in terms of our society's marks of success. Even the church itself has been caught up in our culture's way of evaluating success. Pastors may well measure their own success in terms of the size of their salary, their staff, or their church's membership. Congregations may determine how successful they are by their budgets, their physical plants, their staffs, or the number or social status of their members. None of us is immune to the signs of success that our culture designates.

There is a place for strategizing and planning for goals in human life. If we wish to travel somewhere, a pragmatic approach that looks for maps, itineraries, reservations, and so forth obviously is a good thing. If we have the goal of being healthier, we need to learn about exercise, diet, and relaxation. All of this makes sense. But the most significant relationships in human life cannot be dealt with pragmatically, and yet this is often the temptation. Imagine that a young woman wishes to have a child *in order to*—the signal words of a pragmatic approach—keep her boyfriend or show the world she is an adult. The child has now become a means to an end. What happens if the child does not do what it has been conceived to do? The boyfriend leaves, the society does not treat her the way she expected, and the child becomes for her a burden. Children cannot be viewed primarily as a means to an end. They are ends in themselves. Imagine a person who befriends another because it seems the other person might prove useful in the future. What kind of a friendship is that? Imagine a woman who marries a particular man because his position gives her status. She may find it no longer reasonable to stay with him if he becomes ill, or loses his job in an economic downturn. Imagine the man who marries a particular woman because she is beautiful, only to have her become less attractive in his eyes as the years go by. We cannot treat other human beings pragmatically without compromising both their humanity and our own.

Slavery was an egregious example of viewing other human beings as objects to be used. The slave's purpose was economic. It was unthinkable to free a slave who was economically valuable. Slave families could not be kept together when economics dictated that one of them be sold. The weak could not be cared for because it was not economical. All of this now seems to us a completely distorted view. Yet we run the same danger in many of our contemporary relationships. The search for economic or social status can lead to terrible actions against those who stand in our way. In the context, however, such actions may seem reasonable.

Most of us are aware of the stark contrast between the gospel and the way we measure our lives. We may assume that it is only the excesses of our own culture that make it so difficult to live on the basis of the gospel. We may even wish that we lived in an earlier time, when it would have been easier to be a fully dedicated Christian. It is true that we probably have more difficulty than would those in a more traditional society, where the choices of the individual were extremely limited. A "self-made man" is not something ancient Israel or the Middle Ages would have understood. There were too many social "givens" for individuals to take very much credit for what they had done with their lives. Whom they married, their employment, where they lived—all were generally determined by their tribes, their fathers, or the nobles who controlled the land.

At the same time, we must not exaggerate how easy it might have been for the first Christians to have understood and followed the way Jesus outlines in the strange verses mentioned above (Matthew 6:19 and 20:26; Luke 9:23). In fact, Jesus seemed to spend a great deal of time pointing out that his own disciples had not yet comprehended what he was saying. The gospel, at its heart, runs contrary to human wisdom in any society. It strikes at the core of our sinfulness in any age and in any culture. It cuts the nerve of self-seeking for prestige, for security, or for acceptance. It assumes that our security and status are to be sought in God. All other sources of security and status are by definition idols. That is more radical than most of us care to be. We would prefer to hedge our bets: trust God for security in the hereafter but be clear to have enough wealth and power, enough children or pension plans, enough status and security, and enough success (however defined) to feel safe in this world. But that is precisely what the words of Jesus are opposing. True discipleship demands nothing more and nothing less than our entire trust in God, holding nothing back.

For the Reformers in the sixteenth century this wholehearted trust was the meaning of faith. It is not pragmatic and it does not necessarily lead to anything that the world would recognize as success. John Calvin, the sixteenth-century Reformer, described this in terms of "glory," another way of speaking of prestige and success. He wrote that we are to be like planets that reflect the glory of the sun. We do not have the power to be the sun, but can only shine by reflected glory. Our task as human beings is to glorify God, not ourselves. If we do this, then we shine by the reflected glory of God. Our sinfulness leads us to try to glorify ourselves, with perhaps a bit for God. That clearly will not do, and it means we have made idols out of ourselves. We are to glorify God because God is God, not for anything we may receive. We are to be creatures who recognize their Creator.[2] Not even salvation can be viewed as a quid pro quo act, as though we trust in God and therefore, in return,

God gives us salvation. Calvin, in response to a letter Cardinal Sadolet wrote urging the citizens of Geneva to return to the Roman Catholic Church:

> [S]ince...it certainly is the duty of a Christian man to ascend higher than merely to seek and secure the salvation of his own soul. I therefore believe that there is no man imbued with true piety, who will not regard as in poor taste that long and detailed exhortation to a zeal for heavenly life, which occupies a man entirely concerned with himself.[3]

If we view faith pragmatically, then we have turned faith into a work, something we do in order to gain God's favor. Such a view also turns God into an idol, one we placate in order to gain the favor we wish, something we seek to control by our actions. This is not the relationship we are called to have with our Creator and Redeemer.

We may assume that since we worship the proper God and have no visible idols around us our situation and our temptations are totally unlike those of ancient Israel. However, a close look at Israel's history may demonstrate a greater similarity than we imagined, and thereby help us better understand our own situation.

OTHER BIBLICAL VOICES

(1) Judges 2:11-17

The book of Judges describes the time between Israel's entering Canaan, the land of promise, and the establishment of the monarchy. There were other people living in the land—the Canaanites— who worshiped the Baals. We find a summary of the situation in Judges 2:11-17:

> Then the Israelites did what was evil in the sight of the LORD and worshiped the Baals; and they abandoned the LORD, the God of their ancestors, who had brought them out of the land of Egypt; they followed other gods, from among the gods of the peoples who were all around them, and bowed down to them; and they provoked the LORD to anger. They abandoned the LORD, and worshiped Baal and the Astartes. So the anger of the LORD was kindled against Israel, and he gave them over to plunderers who plundered them, and he sold them into the power of their ene-

mies all around, so that they could no longer withstand their enemies. Whenever they marched out, the hand of the LORD was
against them to bring misfortune, as the LORD had warned them
and sworn to them; and they were in great distress.

Then the LORD raised up judges, who delivered them out of the
power of those who plundered them. Yet they did not listen even
to their judges; for they lusted after other gods and bowed down
to them. They soon turned aside from the way in which their
ancestors had walked, who had obeyed the commandments of
the LORD; they did not follow their example.

It might seem that Israel simply decided to worship other gods,
taking over the habits of the people already living in the land, but
it is more complicated than that. It is not just a religious matter.
Think of who the Israelites were. They had just entered a "land
flowing with milk and honey." They had been slaves in Egypt, then
wanderers in the wilderness, and now they were living in a new
land. Perhaps in the journey through the wilderness they had had
some flocks, but they could not have been farmers. Now they have
come into a land where they have settled and begun an agricultural
life. For this, they must follow the example of their neighbors. So if
a neighbor says that to get good crops you should offer a sacrifice
to the god who controls the land, you probably would do it. Today,
we make a distinction between religion and farming. Ancient peoples did not. Religion was partly for the purpose of having good
crops, of being sure the flocks were productive. Ceremonies that
have to do with planting crops were religious, yes, but they were
also simply the way one farmed. Israel wanted good crops, so they
followed the example of the people who knew how to do this. It
would be quite easy for them to assume that as long as they continued to worship the God of Israel they could also add these other
ceremonies that had to do with how to live in this new land. [4]

That is not very different from our own practices. As long as we
continue to worship God, which we do on Sunday, we assume we
need to live our business or social lives on the basis of what works,
what lets us "get ahead." We assume that to be a Christian means
that we obey the law, we do not do illegal things in business, we
are honest, and so forth. In social life we are polite and considerate.
But within those limitations we generally carry out business in the
same way any other honest person would. Our friendships and

social life are like any other decent citizen's. Our business life is geared to getting ahead, to making a profit. Our social life also assumes we make friends on the same basis as others of our social status. We may not have statues of gods that show what we are doing, but the result is really quite the same. We learn how to live our business and social life from the surrounding society and not from the gospel.

We need to have some sympathy for the Israelites and see how easy it was for them to pick up the practices of their new condition, for only then can we see the parallels in our own lives. It is not the statues of gods that is the problem. It is living life on the basis of competing values, as though the God of Israel did not also govern agriculture or business or whatever else seems to require a different way. It is the closing off of the true God into a "religious" sphere, so that the rest of our lives can be lived on a "practical" basis as though the true God required totally impractical things. Yet what God requires may well be "impractical" in terms of the values of the society around us. That is precisely the problem. That is the conflict between the gospel and the culture.

When we read passages such as this one from Judges we might assume there is a quid pro quo even here: God will protect them if they are obedient. God is saying that life will be good if they obey, and disastrous if they disobey. If this is pragmatism, it is so on a grand scale. It means trusting God for everything, and not hedging one's bets by trusting other powers or values as well. Israel was in a covenant with God, and the heart of that covenant was that only God was to be trusted in all things—in agriculture, in business, in family life, in social life, in health, in international relations, in all of life and even in death. One could not worship the true God and then trust also in some other set of values for other areas of life. Israel had a difficult time learning this, and we do as well. Our relationship to God is a covenantal one. Our temptations are, in very basic ways, the same as Israel's.

(2) Matthew 20:1-16 and Luke 15:11-32

The text we will deal with is in the middle of chapter 20 of Matthew. However, there is a parable that precedes that passage, which in itself is helpful in interpreting the latter section. We therefore will look at the parable in its own right and as a helpful prelude to the passage selected for the sermon. The parable concerns the laborers who are called at various times of the day to work in a landowner's vineyard. The owner has work to be done and goes to what amounts to an ancient day-labor pool. He hires some early in the morning, others at nine o'clock, and still others at noon and three o'clock. Finally, at five o'clock he hires more workers. He has agreed to pay the first workers the usual daily wage, and promises the later ones that he will pay them fairly. When the time comes— evidently about six o'clock—to pay the workers, he gives them each the full wage for a day. Those who had been working in the vineyard for the whole day found it totally unfair that they should receive the same wage as those who worked only one hour.

Most of us probably would agree with those who worked the full day. Isn't it unfair that those who worked probably ten to twelve hours at hard, physical labor in the heat of the day should receive no more than those who came at five o'clock and worked one hour in the cool of the late afternoon? The response of the landowner is interesting:

> Friend, I am doing you no wrong; did you not agree with me for the usual daily wage? Take what belongs to you and go; I choose to give to this last the same as I give to you. Am I not allowed to do what I choose with what belongs to me? Or are you envious because I am generous? So the last will be first, and the first will be last. (Matthew 20:13-16)

The early workers surely felt they were more successful than those not hired. They had achieved their goal of a day's work and would get a day's pay. That was success in comparison to those who were left with no work. The landowner then hired these unsuccessful workers and made them equal. Needless to say, this is not a form of labor relations we are likely to find in our world today. It obviously was not typical in ancient Israel, which is precisely the point the parable is making. The way God deals with us is not at all the way we usually deal with one another. Our temptation is to try to apply to God—and to expect God to apply to us—the same practices as our society holds. That is one of the ways we tailor the gospel to fit our culture.

Perhaps our difficulty with this passage is its economic language. We know about wages and working hours. We have a clear sense of what is fair in this regard. However, the same point is made by the more familiar parable of the prodigal son (Luke 15:11-32). Here again is one—the older son—who has spent his whole life in obedient service to his father. Now the younger son, the prodigal, returns. He has wasted not only his inheritance, but also years of his life. He has not served his father until what amounts to the last hour. Yet the father celebrates the return of the younger son, and the older son cannot understand it. The older son and the early workers of the vineyard parable agree in their dislike of the father's/landowner's actions toward the younger son/late-coming workers. We seem to have an easier time dealing with the parable that puts the issue in family terms rather than in an economic idiom. We can understand that a parent continues to love even a disobedient child. It is harder to think of an employer showing the same generosity.

Both the early workers and the older brother evidently thought they had gained a great advantage. Both felt they were more successful than the latecomers, whether other workers or the prodigal brother. They had worked harder and longer, and should be rewarded. But their reward has been taken from them. They are no better than the less successful ones. Why struggle to get ahead when in the long run it does not matter? What is the reward we are to expect when we serve God faithfully? Surely if we serve all of our lives, that should count for something!

Salvation—a close, loving relationship with God that begins now and lasts eternally—is the ultimate goal of human beings. It is the great gift of God. The person who is able to enjoy such a relationship for eighty years has really received more that is of ultimate value than the eighty-year-old who undergoes a deathbed conversion and therefore has only a few days in this life to enjoy that relationship. The older brother of the prodigal has lived with his father all of these years, but evidently for him it was labor, a duty, a task, not a joyful relationship that was an end in itself, a relationship that was its own reward. The early workers were given a good day's work with a good day's wage. All day long they knew that they were secure at least for the time being. The later workers had spent the day worrying whether they would ever find labor. They had been looking for work, and surely they needed it in order to take care of their families. Probably by five o'clock they were very discouraged and worried about how they would manage. They had been idle, but their idleness was not laziness. They had sought work, as they make clear to the landowner. Which would we rather have been? Had we been given the choice the evening before—come at six in the morning or five in the evening, and the wage will be the same—perhaps then we might have chosen the easier way. But that was not what happened. Those who worked all day had a security that the others lacked.

A relationship with God in Christ is its own reward. It is not something we have earned. It is not a mark of our successful striving. If someone else comes to such a relationship late in life, there is no reason for us to think how unfair it is that they receive the same as we do. The relationship is its reward, and we have enjoyed it for years longer than the other person. The other may regret how much time has been lost, but we can rejoice in how much time we have been given. We have gained much and lost nothing. The only way we can miss this point is if we are indeed like that older brother who looks at his time with his father as work and not joy.

Salvation is not a reward for anything we do. We have not earned it. It is a relationship that God has initiated, an opportunity that God has opened to us. All who are related to God in this saving manner are enjoying the same thing, whether they have come late or early to such a relationship.[5]

(3) Psalm 73

The psalmist presents us with a brief history of how he has learned what really matters in his relationship with God. He had been told, and he believed, that "truly God is good to the upright." That is the beginning of the psalm. But by the next verse it appears that he has forgotten that truth. He saw the wicked lead easy lives, without the kind of hardship that he and others who sought to be obedient to God suffered. The wicked prospered and the good did not. The psalmist almost decided it was useless to be obedient to God. Up to this point in the psalm it would seem that the author had viewed his relationship to God in quite pragmatic terms, and it had not worked:

> All in vain I have kept my heart clean
> and washed my hands in innocence.
> For all day long I have been plagued,
> and am punished every morning.
> (Psalm 73:13-14)

But then the psalmist goes into the sanctuary and begins to realize the true situation. The wicked are easily ruined when what they trust in is removed. The faithful, however, trust in that which cannot be removed. Understanding this, the psalmist repents his earlier anger:

> When my soul was embittered,
>> when I was pricked in heart,
> I was stupid and ignorant;
>> I was like a brute beast toward you.
> Nevertheless I am continually with you;
>> you hold my right hand.
> You guide me with your counsel,
>> and afterward you will receive me with honor.
> Whom have I in heaven but you?
>> And there is nothing on earth that I desire
>> other than you. (Psalm 73:21-25)

The psalmist has learned what the older brother of the prodigal son and the early workers in the vineyard had not yet learned: the relationship with God, who in the parables is paralleled with the father and the owner, is what matters. Those who treasure that relationship know that what they have is far more valuable than anything else.

BACK TO THE TEXT: MATTHEW 20:17-28

This passage occurs immediately after the parable of the vineyard owner discussed above, and needs to be understood in that context. This narrative has three sections. In the first, Jesus announces to the Twelve that when they get to Jerusalem "the Son of Man will be handed over to the chief priests and scribes, and they will condemn him to death; then they will hand him over to the Gentiles to be mocked and flogged and crucified; and on the third day he will be raised" (Matthew 20:18-19). That is a succinct statement of what will happen during Holy Week. The last words about being raised on the third day are quite positive, but everything before that is very bleak.

Immediately following this statement to the Twelve, the mother of the sons of Zebedee came to Jesus to make her request, which is the second section of the narrative. She clearly was not part of the Twelve who heard what Jesus had just said, but her sons had been. Her request to Jesus is, "Declare that these two sons of mine will sit, one at your right hand and one at your left, in your kingdom" (Matthew 20:21). This does seem presumptuous for the mother. It is as though she is saying, "Those who have been with you all this time surely will have privileged places in your kingdom. I want my two sons to have the most privileged places of all!" We do not know what her sons thought of her words, but in verse 24 we are told that "when the ten heard it, they were angry with the two brothers." So probably the sons were in accord with their mother.

Jesus addressed the sons directly, not the mother, asking if they can drink his cup—that is, share his fate, particularly his death. The same image of the cup is used again in Matthew when Jesus, in the Garden of Gethsemane, agrees to drink the cup God has appointed (Matthew 26:39, 42).[6] In this earlier section he has just described his fate—that he will be condemned to death. The brothers see no problem with sharing that fate. Jesus noted that he does not think they really know what they are asking (Matthew 20:22). It is almost as though they were so intent on considering what positions they might hold that they had not really heard what Jesus said about the necessary suffering before such glory. Perhaps they were thinking about the kind of kingdom they were used to in this world. Jesus then tells them that they will indeed drink his cup, but that Jesus himself has no authority to grant them privileged seats in the kingdom; his Father has arranged all that (Matthew 20:23).

The sons of Zebedee and their mother seem to be viewing the relationship with Jesus on the basis of what it will gain for the sons. The other ten were angry, but they may well have been viewing the matter in the same way and wanted those seats for themselves.[7] Jesus then addressed the Twelve and made very clear that their desire for privileged seats, signs of status in the coming kingdom, was totally inappropriate. They were dealing with the kingdom of God as though it were just another earthly kingdom that worked on the usual principles.

> "You know that the rulers of the Gentiles lord it over them, and their great ones are tyrants over them. It will not be so among you; but whoever wishes to be great among you must be your servant, and whoever wishes to be first among you must be your

slave; just as the Son of Man came not to be served but to serve, and to give his life a ransom for many." (Matthew 20:25-28)

The term for the word *serve* used here is the Greek verb *diakoneo*. It has particular reference to serving at a table as a waiter or maid. While the image of a ruler in an earthly kingdom is someone whom others hasten to serve, in God's reign the most important people are those who do the serving, not those who are served.[8] Status in the kingdom of God is based on service. Why bother achieving status if all it means is that you have to serve others? Surely it is for the purpose of having others serve you. Why would the mother of the sons of Zebedee want such status for her children? Why would the sons want it? Why would the other ten be angry at the two sons of Zebedee, if they all understood what Jesus was telling them? The mother would be offering her sons as the slaves of all, the sons would be agreeing that this is what they want, and the other ten would be content to let them be such servants or else would wish to outdo them in service. But the mother and sons are hoping for status, not service, and so are the other ten angry disciples, as we see from Jesus' words to them all.

Status is not something one would seek in the kingdom. Jesus gives his own life as an example. He has just said that he is going to die a terrible death. Now he shows that this death is not to be avoided, because it is a way of serving others. The disciples have yet to learn what this means. In fact, it will not be until after the Resurrection and the coming of the Holy Spirit that they will truly be able to understand and embrace the cup that Jesus has offered them.

In this narrative the disciples still view their relationship with Jesus in pragmatic terms: "What will it give me in the future?" They do not understand that their friendship with Jesus—and his with them—is all the reward they need. After the Resurrection, when that friendship continues even beyond death, they will understand. And then they will indeed be able to suffer and endure all things, even with joy, because their relationship to Jesus, and through him to God, continues to be the greatest blessing in the world.

In the early church, when Christians were a persecuted minority within the Roman Empire, there were many martyrs. The term "martyr" is derived from a Greek word meaning "witness," as in one who testifies in a law court. For Christians, it came to mean one who witnessed to the faith even to the point of death. The early martyrs believed that in their suffering and death they were actually joined to Christ, so that it was he who suffered in them. Their deaths were the ultimate seal that their relationship to Christ was so overwhelmingly positive that nothing else compared to it, not even a comfortable life without suffering. To be separated from Christ would have been greater suffering than the terrible trials they had to endure as martyrs.

All of this the disciples still had to learn. They did not yet know what Jesus really meant by God's kingdom. They still compared it to the earthly kingdoms they knew. They did not yet really understand who Jesus was and what his death and resurrection would accomplish. We can therefore understand why they might seek the kind of status that the mother of the sons of Zebedee sought.

Our situation is different. We do know what happened during Holy Week. We stand on this side of Easter and Pentecost. Yet in so many ways we are there with those disciples, headed to Jerusalem and still not understanding how different things should be. The church is the community of those who should understand the difference Jesus has made in the world. The life of the kingdom has actually begun, and we are its witnesses. Our communal life as the church should exhibit this new life in which status is totally reversed. Yet our congregational life probably is little different than that of any other group in our society in terms of giving or seeking status.

Based on what the other passages we have looked at in this chapter tell us, our failure to embody this radically different life probably shows that we have allowed the values of the surrounding culture to alter the gospel message. We have permitted a desire for success in terms our culture can understand to determine how we should live. As we have seen, this is a form of idolatry. At the same time, we have devalued the importance of our relationship to God, trying to see what it can do for us in comparison to other values. Such valuations, however, show that our relationship to God is not what it should be. If it were, the joy of it would keep us from seeking other security.

Joy is the hallmark of God's presence in our lives. Where joy exists, nothing else is needed or can be valued more highly. We have reached the goal, and in that Christian sense we are successful, even in the midst of persecution or apparent failure.

PREACHING THIS TEXT TODAY

The goal of the sermon is to raise the question of what values we live by—those of the surrounding society, or those of faith that trusts in God for our security. The task of the preacher is to help the congregation see how much like those disciples we are. For that purpose, it would be helpful to use the Judges passage as the Old Testament lesson, and then show how similar the disciples are to ancient Israel. The parallel could be done very quickly, showing that Israel, the disciples, and we take our cues from the surrounding society on how to live in this world. This would require some emphasis on the kind of society we live in, and how easy it is to assume as normative the marks of success that surround us. We try to combine some of the values of the gospel with some of the values of the society, but that is precisely what ancient Israel was doing. Churches as well as individual Christians continue to perform these dangerous combinations.

Then the preacher must clarify what Jesus is calling us to do and to be. It is not simply a negative: giving up things. It is a positive: a relationship with God in Christ that is worth more than anything else. It is the beginning of the kingdom, of eternal life, here and now. It would be useful to compare the disciples in this account with the fearless apostles who later risked even life itself. What was the difference? Because of Easter and the power of the Holy Spirit, they had finally understood what Jesus was teaching them. They knew the joy and the power that came from trusting God completely. Their relationship to God was an experienced reality. That should be the goal of our Christian lives as well. We so often look at the negative—what we will lose in the way of success that the world understands. We need to look at the positive—lives of great joy that nothing or no one can take away.

It would be good if the preacher raised the question of how the congregation views its own success. What does it mean to be a successful church? How can the congregation help its members look seriously at the way we all live our lives, both individually and as a congregation? Such an emphasis could be useful shortly before

Lent so that some special studies could go on during the Lenten season, leading to a renewed dedication at Easter.

If the congregation's liturgy permits it, Psalm 73 could be used after the sermon as a prayer. If not, it could be used wherever a psalm is to be read during the service.

SUGGESTED READING

Boring, M. Eugene. "Matthew," in *The New Interpreter's Bible,* vol. 8. Nashville: Abingdon Press, 1995.

Foulkes, Francis. *A Guide to St. Matthew's Gospel.* International Study Guide. London: SPCK, 2001.

Hare, Douglas R. A. *Matthew.* Interpretation: A Bible Commentary for Teaching and Preaching. Louisville: John Knox Press, 1993.

Senior, Donald. *Matthew.* Abingdon New Testament Commentaries. Nashville: Abingdon Press, 1998.

CHAPTER FIVE

The God of Vengeance

THE TEXT

Romans 12:14–13:4

Bless those who persecute you; bless and do not curse them.
Rejoice with those who rejoice, weep with those who weep. Live
in harmony with one another; do not be haughty, but associate
with the lowly; do not claim to be wiser than you are. Do not
repay anyone evil for evil, but take thought for what is noble in
the sight of all. If it is possible, so far as it depends on you, live
peaceably with all. Beloved, never avenge yourselves, but leave
room for the wrath of God; for it is written, "Vengeance is mine,
I will repay, says the Lord." No, "if your enemies are hungry,
feed them; if they are thirsty, give them something to drink; for
by doing this you will heap burning coals on their heads." Do
not be overcome by evil, but overcome evil with good.

Let every person be subject to the governing authorities; for
there is no authority except from God, and those authorities that
exist have been instituted by God. Therefore whoever resists
authority resists what God has appointed, and those who resist
will incur judgment. For rulers are not a terror to good conduct,
but to bad. Do you wish to have no fear of the authority? Then
do what is good, and you will receive its approval; for it is
God's servant for your good. But if you do what is wrong, you
should be afraid, for the authority does not bear the sword in
vain! It is the servant of God to execute wrath on the wrongdoer.

THE DIFFICULTY

Our world is filled with violence. Nations rise against nations, and those who had no part in the conflict are driven from their homes. Our newspapers and televisions give us horrifying pictures of families, including children and the elderly, fleeing from ethnic violence, running from the homes they have known all their lives. Often the source of the conflict goes back generations. There has been an endless cycle of each side paying back the other for wrongs done in past generations. Each side seeks vengeance for the actions of the other.

Vengeance: it is a terrible word. It has overtones of hatred, of a drive to get even with those who have wronged us. It is not surprising, then, that we have difficulty with passages in the Bible that speak of our God as a God of vengeance. Surely this is not a term that can be applied to God! Yet the Bible is filled with such verses. We need to look much more clearly at what is meant. Tied to the word *vengeance* is the whole idea of God's involvement in the violence of our world. How can the God of love, the God known in Jesus, also be the God of vengeance?

Early in the history of the church, in the second century, a man named Marcion developed a theology that pitted the God of the Old Testament against the God of Jesus in the New Testament. For Marcion, the God of Israel is of wrath, of law and punishment, of vengeance. The God of the New Testament is of love and forgiveness. The two cannot be reconciled, and therefore we must choose between them. Marcion chose what he understood the New Testament God to be, and dismissed both Israel and the Old Testament as the work of an alien and inferior god. He discovered he had to edit severely much of the New Testament as well. For Marcion, vengeance and love, the demands of righteousness and the message of forgiveness, cannot go together.

In many ways, as we struggle with the understanding of God as a God of vengeance, we are revisiting the conflict that Marcion saw. In the second century, his views were rejected and he was declared a heretic. The church declared that our God revealed in both Old and New Testaments is a God of righteousness and love, a God who gives us the law and who forgives our sins, a God who is both judging and forgiving. There is a place for the word *vengeance* in our understanding of a loving and merciful God.

The Word Vengeance

The root of our English word *vengeance* picks up nuances of both the Hebrew and the Greek terms it is used to translate. However, for most of us the meaning is negative. We forget that in English both *vengeance* and *vindication* come from the same Latin root. We receive into English the meaning of the Hebrew and Greek terms through Latin. The avenger is one who brings revenge, yes, but also the one who brings vindication. For us *vindication* is a positive word. It implies being shown to be innocent or being defended against enemies who would defame or defeat us. *Vindication* is good, but *vengeance* seems negative. We rarely use the word *avenger* because it seems violent; and yet the word *vindicator* has no violent connotations but really means the same thing. So the word *vengeance* must be understood both as judgment and punishment, and as bringing justice to the wrongfully treated. In God's hands, vengeance seeks to accomplish justice, vindicating the oppressed and judging the oppressor. Such action is not a denial of God's love but rather a means for demonstrating it.[1] God's vengeance therefore does not include the unforgiving storing up of grievances that we associate with human vengeance. God is not vindictive.

How can conflicts between peoples ever be overcome if there is no forgiveness, if there is only a ceaseless paying back, causing new injury that leads to new acts of revenge? Each side considers itself justified in its new acts of violence, and each act gives the other side reason for its own violence. This may be human vengeance— vindictive but not creating justice. However, it is not what happens when God is the avenger. God does not store up all of our past sins, never forgetting them, never forgiving. God seeks reconciliation and a new beginning, even when God punishes. In the words of the psalmist: "As far as the east is from the west, so far [God] removes our transgressions from us" (Psalm 103:12). Yet the psalmist recognizes that though God is angry about sin and injustice, God "will not always accuse, nor will he keep his anger forever" (Psalm 103:9). God's vengeance seeks reconciliation, forgiveness; it restores or establishes a loving relationship. Human vengeance seems to have no way to a new beginning. It just goes on and on in the cycle of violence, each side blaming the other, with no way to end it. Although we may use the word *vengeance* in both cases, we need to understand there is a great difference. Marcion was wrong. A love that cares nothing about justice, a love that sees righteousness as unimportant is not the love God has for us.

Throughout the Bible, God's love is understood to be like a parent's love. God brings up humanity just as a parent tries to bring up a child. It is necessary to set limits, to punish, to let a child sometimes experience the consequences of bad decisions. A human parent does not always make wise decisions, nor does a human parent have control over all the variables. But God has the ultimate control of the future, of life and death, and life beyond death. God's concern and love are for the whole creation. It is in that context that we need to look at how God's vengeance, and the violence of our world are intertwined.

It would be far better if there were no violence and if all peoples were open to following the will of God. But that is not the kind of world in which we are living. We live in the midst of a rebellious world, one that has turned against God's ways. Yet even our violent world is not out from under the governance of God. What mattered for ancient Israel and still matters for God's people today is the absolute confidence that even in a violent world, God is still in control. God is still God. God is still seeking to turn the wayward creation to the paths of righteousness.

Even those who oppose God unwillingly serve God's goals of justice and righteousness. This was the pattern in the case of the destruction of Israel by Assyria in the eighth century BCE, and in the capture of Judah by Babylon two centuries later. The prophets had said that the destruction was coming upon the nation because the nation had turned away from God and had been unrighteous in its actions. When such destruction came, if the people believed the prophets, then they felt called to repentance. If they did not believe the prophets, then their interpretation was likely to be that God was treating them unfairly or had abandoned them. God was not causing another nation to be violent, but rather using this violence to judge Israel and bring the nation back to faithfulness. In due time the violent nation would also be judged.

The prophet Isaiah describes the way God dealt with faithless Israel:

Ah, Assyria, the rod of my anger—
    the club in their hands is my fury!
Against a godless nation I send him,
    and against the people of my wrath I command
        him,
to take spoil and seize plunder,
    and to tread them down like the mire of the
        streets.
But this is not what he intends,
    nor does he have this in mind;
    but it is in his heart to destroy....

When the Lord has finished all his work on Mount Zion and on Jerusalem, he will punish the arrogant boasting of the king of Assyria and his haughty pride. (Isaiah 10:5-7, 12)

God was angry with Israel. God desired righteousness in the community of the covenant people. For other nations they were to be a model of how God wishes us to live. By their unrighteousness the people of God were failing in their vocation. God used the existing violence of others to call them back. Violence alone would not be enough; it required also the voice of the prophets interpreting what was happening. We can say that God was taking vengeance on Israel. We can say that later God would take vengeance on Assyria in order to vindicate Israel. The words are the same: *vengeance* and *vindication*. In both cases God was seeking to do justice and righteousness in an unjust situation, using the violence there for redemptive purposes.

OTHER BIBLICAL VOICES

(1) Genesis 4:8-15

After Cain killed Abel, God punished him by sending him away from the land and told him that the ground would no longer be fruitful for him because his brother's blood had been received by the earth. When Cain expressed his fear that he would now be fair game for anyone to kill, "the LORD said to him, '... Whoever kills Cain will suffer a sevenfold vengeance.' And the LORD put a mark on Cain, so that no one who came upon him would kill him" (Genesis 4:15). There would be consequences for killing Abel. Justice needed to be done. But God had punished Cain. It was

God's vengeance, and no one should carry out human vengeance. The first hearers of this story may have assumed some member of Abel's family would act as avenger. However, God protected Cain from such retribution even as Cain suffered punishment from God.

Ambrose, the great fourth-century bishop of Milan, commented on this passage in relation to capital punishment. Before he became bishop, Ambrose had been the civil governor of Milan under the Roman emperor. He well knew the need to protect society from criminals, and the role of the civil authority to carry this out. His faith allowed him to see that even in the midst of such necessity Christians ought not to lose sight of God's work of redemption. He wrote:

> From the point of view of our faith, no one ought to slay a person who in the course of nature still would have time for repentance up to the very moment of his death. A guilty man—provided a premature punishment had not deprived him of life—could well procure forgiveness by redeeming himself by an act of repentance, however belated.[2]

Society must protect itself from those who would destroy the community by their criminality. But God's prerogatives in terms of vengeance limit what human beings can do in response to evil. At least those in the community of faith should understand these limits. I will return to this theme later.

(2) Psalm 137:7-9

The captive Jews, taken into exile in Babylon, have been asked by their oppressors to sing one of the Jewish songs. The response of the Jews is that they cannot do that under the circumstance. Instead, they ask God to avenge their suffering. The conclusion of the psalm includes words that most of us have difficulty reciting:

> Remember, O LORD, against the Edomites
>   the day of Jerusalem's fall,
> how they said, "Tear it down! Tear it down!
>   Down to its foundations!"
> O daughter Babylon, you devastator!
>   Happy shall they be who pay you back
>   what you have done to us!
> Happy shall they be who take your little ones
>   and dash them against the rock! (Psalm 137:7-9)

Killing infants by throwing them against rocks in front of their parents is hardly a wish we feel comfortable expressing. At the same time, it is a natural, human response to those who probably just had the same thing done against them. Such revenge in kind is ever present. The desire for revenge creates a violent cycle.

Human beings have done terrible things to one another. Especially in war horrible actions occur. We have seen it in our own day. The captive Jews might have been hoping God would bring the retribution they desired. It does not mean that they were about to carry out the violence themselves. Perhaps by speaking such wishes to God they hoped that God would take care of it. In any case, it is a difficult though understandable response. It is clear the desire for revenge haunts human relationships, especially on the level of nations.

(3) Deuteronomy 32:34-43

This scripture is part of the closing verses of the Song of Moses, a recapitulation of Israel's history and God's response placed in the mouth of Moses. The earlier verses show God's great care for Israel, particularly during the time in the desert. God gave them a fertile land, but Israel's response to this was to spurn God and turn to the idols of the land. God therefore punished them by permitting foreign nations to rise against them and by letting the Israelites be defeated. But God was concerned that these conquering nations might suppose their victories would show that they themselves were strong, with their not knowing that it was the God of Israel who let them succeed. Therefore God caused the enemies of Israel to fall before Israel.

In these brief verses, the term *vengeance* occurs three times, along with *vindicate* and *avenge*. The most famous use of the word *vengeance* is in 32:35: "Vengeance is mine, and recompense." This time God's vengeance on the foreign nation will bring vindication for Israel, whereas earlier God's vengeance had been on Israel because of its sin. In both cases, what is important is that vengeance remains the prerogative of God. It is a recompense, but one only that God can give. God's purpose is to bring Israel back to faithfulness and to show the other nations that before the true God they have no power.

This verse, in a slightly different translation, is quoted twice in the New Testament: once in Romans 12:19, to which we shall turn more extensively later, and the other time in Hebrews 10:30. In the first instance, the verse points to God's vengeance against the persecutors of the church. In the Hebrews passage, God's vengeance is against Christians who fall away during a time of persecution. As in the Song of Moses, God's vengeance can be against those within as well as those outside the community of faith. In both cases it is the evidence of God's wrath against sin but also the means of overcoming that sin. We as the church can be the subjects both of God's vengeance and God's vindication—remember, the root words are the same.

With this brief look at the biblical view of God's vengeance, I will return to the basic text of this study.

BACK TO THE TEXT: ROMANS 12:14–13:4

For many of us, Romans 12 is both familiar and strange. It is familiar because it contains many frequently quoted verses or phrases. It is unfamiliar because often we do not see the passage as a whole, and therefore lose many of the connections among the more familiar words. Paul's reasoning here is quite closely argued. It is based on all that he has said before, and now he is applying it directly to the life of Christians in Rome. In verse 9 he emphasizes that genuine love is the ultimate character of a Christian. In verses 9-13, he shows what this means for their life together as the church.

In verse 14, he indicates that love cannot be turned off at the boundary of the Christian community. It must show itself in the dealings of Christians with the wider world, with neighbors who are not Christian. Above all, it is to be seen in the attitude of Christians toward their persecutors.

There are two particular difficulties with this passage. First, as we have seen, the word *vengeance* in English carries connotations of hatred and violence, of getting even. We need to be clear what the nuances of the word's meaning are in the original languages so that we do not read into the text elements not originally meant. Second, even when we do understand the meaning, what is demanded of us as Christians in this passage seems humanly impossible. Paul's argument probably would be that humanly it is indeed impossible.

Only those who are part of the new creation, those who have begun to be raised with Christ, those in whom the Holy Spirit dwells, can begin to love this extraordinarily. No amount of word study can remove this difficulty.

As I noted in the first chapter, we so often weaken the meaning of the word *enemies* that the commands to love our enemies seems easy enough to accomplish. We forget that in the earliest Christian community, where enemies were quite real and the possibility of persecution constant, love for enemies was considered the highest achievement of faith. It was a love that encompassed the whole world and not just friends. It was a love that paralleled God's own love. It was love that, unlike faith and hope, would never pass away (1 Corinthians 13:8, 13).

Paul begins this section with the words "Bless those who persecute you; bless and do not curse them" (12:14). There are overtones here of many other passages, including the words of Jesus in Matthew 5:44 and Luke 6:27-28 about loving enemies. We find a similar sentiment about blessing and cursing in James 3:9-10. In the latter passage, the author is not stressing love to enemies, but rather that it is impossible for the same mouth to utter both blessings and cursing. If the Christian is truly loving, then love toward others is what must issue forth. Such love cannot mean cursing the other, no matter how much they are persecutors. That is precisely the point Paul is making here. If our love is genuine, if it is based on all that God has done for us, if it is the result of the transformed life that makes us part of the new creation, then loving even our enemies is the sign of this. We are no longer conformed to the fallen world around us, a world in which it is natural to seek to hurt those who hurt us. Rather, we have been transformed (12:2), and love for all is the result.

The Gospel parallels stress praying for our enemies. Here the task is blessing them. That amounts to the same thing. To bless someone is to pray that God will be good to that person; to curse is to pray that God will punish him or her. The usual human response regarding enemies is to pray that God will avenge us, and therefore punish those who persecute or otherwise harm us. We saw that in the conclusion of Psalm 137. Here the standard is higher: we are not just to stop our own vengeance and pray that God will avenge us. Rather, we are to bless our enemies and pray that God will be good to them. That is a very difficult task indeed. It cuts to the core of the nature of the Christian life. We need to remember that God loved us, even when we were enemies,[3] as Paul had already written in Romans 5:8. Why should we not then assume that God may well love those who are still God's enemies and ours as well? We are called to have the same attitude toward our enemies that God had toward us.

In Romans 12:15-18, Paul calls on Christians to live peaceably with others. Who are these "others"? Are they other Christians, or is he still speaking of those outside the church, those who might be persecutors? There is a difference of opinion about this. It is best to assume that Paul is still speaking about outsiders, since the verses that follow raise the possibility of these "others" being enemies.[4] The Christian community, even in the midst of persecution, is not to withdraw to its own ghetto, avoiding others. They are to treat even their enemies as fellow human beings, rejoicing with their human joys and weeping with them in their sorrows, as much as possible.[5] This rules out rejoicing with them over things that Christians cannot rejoice about. The birth or death of a child; the death of a parent; the illness of a family member; one's recovery from illness; the loss of a job; fire that destroys a home; a happy marriage—these things Christians can respond to on a very human level, whether these "others" are Christians or not, or even if they are our enemies. We are to be their good neighbors even when they are not our good neighbors. We are not to feel superior, but humbly relate to others. We are to support that which is good, especially that which both we and they believe is good. What we are definitely not to do is act toward them with the same evil they give to us. Persecution may still occur, but Christians will have done all that they could to avoid it, while remaining faithful. They are not to return evil for any evil they have received.

In Romans 12:19, Paul quotes the words from the Song of Moses that is in Deuteronomy 32:35: "Vengeance is mine, I will repay, says the Lord." It is a slightly different version from "Vengeance is mine, and recompense," but the meaning is the same. As we have seen, in its original context these words meant that Israel could trust that God would destroy the enemies who attacked Israel, even when those enemies had been used by God to return Israel to faithfulness. In Paul's context, however, the meaning is different.

Christians cannot hope that God will destroy their enemies. They are to pray that God will bless their enemies. One cannot pray God's blessing on them and at the same time pray that God will destroy them. Christians are to hope that this blessing will include changing the hearts of enemies, even making them part of the body of Christ. Meanwhile, Christians are to relate to these present enemies on the basis that they will ultimately become friends.

The Roman Christians are told to "leave room for the wrath of God." It is as though there is a vacuum that violence has created, a vacuum that will either be filled by human vengeance that leads to a terrible cycle, or will be filled by God's vengeance. If human beings carry out their own vengeance, then God's vengeance—one that can be healing—has been hindered, if not prevented. Perhaps even the human avenger will now be the target of God's wrath.

God is a God of vengeance-vindication—making a situation just, doing justice, and bringing judgment, which may mean punishment upon evildoers. God's vengeance is not simply to get even with those who cause hurt. Its purpose is to bring justice to an unjust situation. The passage here implies that we humans are probably unable to judge properly, unable to bring justice to the situation by avenging the wrong. Only God can do that wisely. The emphasis is on the word *mine*. Vengeance belongs to God and not to us. It assumes that God is opposed to evil and injustice; after all, God does punish those who use violence against their neighbors. We can trust that God will do what is best in order to bring about justice, even using the violence of our world to do so.

We can also be certain that leaving the matter in God's hands does not mean being indifferent to evil, ignoring the damage it does. Very often we hear someone say that it is necessary to strike back at evildoers because otherwise justice will not be done and it will seem that evil is winning. If the action of the enemy is criminal, then the civil society has structures for keeping the community safe. As we will see, Paul is very clear about this. Whether enemies are criminals or are problems to us on a more personal level, we need to understand that our failure to pay back those who do evil is not letting evil win, but rather it is leaving to God the role of judge and avenger. We can love our enemies partly because even they are under the providence of God, and God's plans for justice will be fulfilled. At the same time, we are to hope and pray that these current enemies will learn, will come to their senses, will turn to God, and will therefore cease to be evildoers.

In verse 20, Paul turns from Deuteronomy to Proverbs. Quoting from Proverbs 25:21-22, he describes what our actions should be. It is not enough to refrain from evil against our enemies; we are to act positively, doing them good. We are to give them food and drink. These are acts of hospitality that carried great significance in ancient cultures. To give food and drink meant to treat them as friends. It is part of living as the good neighbor even in the midst of enemies. The "heaping burning coals upon their heads" is not a roundabout way of punishing them. Rather, by treating them as friends their hearts may be turned away from evil. "Burning coals" is an interesting phrase. Perhaps it refers to the shame that they may feel in the face of our loving response. Shame causes heat, even to the point of blushing. Our response may cause them to be ashamed of their hostile actions. If so, they are ready to change. If not, it still means that we have done everything we could to turn away their wrath.

The final verse in this passage is the bottom line of all of our dealings with evildoers: we are not to imitate them. No matter what evil they do, we are not to let their evil overcome us. Rather, based on the victory over evil Christ has won for us, we are to overcome evil with good.

In a strange way, imitation is a theme of this passage. We are not to imitate our enemies in the evil they do, in the anger and violence they carry out. Instead, we are to imitate God in the expansiveness of our love. At the same time, we are not to imitate God in vengeance. Vengeance belongs to God and not to us.

What Paul intimates is that Christians should do what is right regardless of what their enemies do. If they act in the same evil way as their enemies act, then they have been overcome by evil. If they do what is right in the face of evil, then within themselves they have overcome evil with good. Their action may also have led to a change within their enemy. Such a change is not the reason for how the Christian acts, though in God's providence it may cause such a change.

We often try to carry out the message of turning the other cheek, of returning good for evil, of not hating our enemies, but find it difficult, if not impossible. We ask how our action can possibly do any good. Would we not accomplish more by striking back? That might at least convey some kind of message to the tormentor. Paul's words— and the words of so much of Scripture—remind us that our not striking back does not mean that nothing will happen to the enemy. God has said, in Paul's words to the Romans, "Vengeance is mine, I will repay." We are to let go our own need for vengeance, and put it in the hands of One who is far more able to act wisely than we are. Our task is to go on following the path of righteousness, which includes praying that God will bless them.

In some preaching situations it may be necessary to go on to the next few verses, Romans 13:1-5, lest the wrong impression be given. The chapter division makes it appear that a totally new subject begins in chapter 13, but that is not the case. It needs to be clear that the words about vengeance do not take the place of a community's need to protect itself and others from those who could carry out evil. The need of the society to be safe obviously means that criminals must be dealt with. It is no accident that in chapter 13 Paul even says that the civil authority is "the servant of God to execute wrath on the wrongdoer" (v. 4). In other words, God's vengeance that was discussed in chapter 12 may sometimes be exercised by the state, even a non-Christian state (since Paul here is assuming the Roman Empire). The authority of the state does include this aspect of punishment. However, it is very difficult to discern when such civil authority is actually exercising the legitimate actions Paul describes, and when it has become a means for the sort of human vengeance we are warned about in chapter 12. Our discussions of capital punishment and our understandings of the penal system—whether its purpose is rehabilitation or vengeance—depend upon making such a distinction. In a sinful world there must be the authority to punish evildoers and prevent harm to society. At the same time, how Christians view the role of such punishment, along with how they understand the distinction between human and divine vengeance, is a critical matter and needs to be discussed publicly much more clearly than it has been.

The law of ancient Israel, as recorded in the Old Testament, had a place for the punishment of crime and for its prevention. At the same time, particularly in the book of Leviticus, we see an additional understanding. If Israel was to be a covenant community, related to the holy God, then it too was called to exemplary holiness.

There was need to be sure that those who were unholy and who therefore contaminated the whole community were eliminated. The laws were harsh and generally included stoning the offenders to death. The purpose of this action was not only to punish the evildoer but also to restore the holy community to its purity by eliminating those who were unholy, much as the early church understood excommunication.

What probably became clear fairly quickly was that the holy community was not really all that holy, even if you eliminated the blatant law-breakers. By the time of the prophets, it was assumed that the whole society was sinful in God's eyes. This view culminates in the famous passage in John 8:1-11, the account of the woman taken in adultery. However and whenever this story entered the canon—and its placement is historically complex—it is there. Surely part of its meaning is that sin is so embedded in society, even among its religious leaders, that to eliminate all the sinful ones would mean eliminating the whole community.

Whether or not such a rationale was used in the earliest period of Israel's life, today it is not possible to use the holiness or purity of the covenant community as a reason for capital punishment because of the extensive character of sin in all contemporary societies. Even those in civil authority who, in Paul's terms, carry out the wrath of God, cannot presume that by eliminating some evildoers they have thereby eliminated evil from the society.

Vengeance remains God's prerogative. Human societies have civil authorities that are responsible for the safety and good order of the whole community. In some fashion, these authorities do show the wrath of God against evil. At the same time, we, as God's people, are warned not to exact vengeance on our own behalf, but rather to allow God to do so in God's own way and time. Even the desire for vengeance, though understandable, is not to be cherished. Rather, we are to practice righteousness even toward those who hate us. The highest level of such righteousness is to hope and pray that God will turn the hearts of our enemies to repentance and that in the future they will become our friends. It is therefore our task to begin treating them as such even now.

We live in a violent society. The Bible is not an unrealistic book filled with directions for living in a perfect world. The Bible knows about evil and sin, even in the midst of the covenant people. Yet the

Scriptures hold out hope for overcoming evil by righteousness and love and not by more evil. We are to be the means by which the cycle of violence is broken, not those through whom it is continued. How should the Christian live in the midst of such a world? By holding to righteousness and by trusting that God, the Avenger and the Redeemer, is in control. With all of its violence, this is still God's world.

PREACHING THIS TEXT TODAY

There are two points that need to be made, and a third that might be necessary. In what order and with what priority depends upon the situation. The points are, first, the meaning of *vengeance* and its cognate, *vindication*—showing the difference between what is meant in the Bible and what we mean in our common parlance. Second, the human impossibility of blessing enemies, and therefore that such a blessing is a sign of the divine activity, the new creation within a human life. Third, it might be necessary to include the role of the civil government in providing safety and security for the community, a task that need not be at odds with blessing and love toward enemies.

How these issues are ordered depends on what the preacher understands to be crucial to the particular congregation. For instance, in a congregation that is active in justice issues, the task could be reminding activists of the need to love those who oppose their actions as well as those who are the victims the activists seek to aid. The sermon could deal specifically with the role of Christians in public debate about national security over against external enemies, or the penal system. It would probably be best to begin with the role of the civil society as well as the need for Christians to bless the enemies even while the civil government carries out its tasks. This could also be helpful as a topical sermon, not as part of a series, but in the midst of a specific social situation.

If the preacher is concerned that the congregation has a view of God that does not take seriously God's opposition to sin and is not very concerned with justice issues, then a different approach is needed. In such a congregation there may be so much emphasis on God's mercy and love for us as individuals that the holiness and justice of God are overlooked. There seem to be many Christians today who find any emphasis on judgment to be a contradiction to love, just as Marcion did in the ancient church. Such a congregation may have difficulty with the concept of God's vengeance. It would need to be shown that this is an integral part of Scripture, both in the Old and the New Testaments. It would also need to be pointed out that we ourselves in the church could be the objects of God's vengeance even though we remain objects of God's love. If this were the direction of the sermon, then it might not be necessary to continue the text into Romans 13.

In either possible direction of the sermon, it needs to be emphasized that blessing our enemies is only possible if we leave vengeance to God.

SUGGESTED READING

Candish, Robert S. *Studies in Romans 12: The Christian's Sacrifice and Service of Praise.* Grand Rapids: Kregel Publications, 1989.

Cranfield, C. E. B. *Commentary on Romans 12–13.* Scottish Journal of Theology Occasional Paper No. 12. Edinburgh: Oliver and Boyd, 1965.

Dawn, Marva. *The Hilarity of Community: Romans 12 and How to Be the Church.* Grand Rapids: Wm. B. Eerdmans Publishing Company, 1992.

Forell, George Wolfgang. *Reflections on Romans 12–15.* Philadelphia: Fortress Press, 1975.

Wright, N. T. "The Letter to the Romans," in *The New Interpreter's Bible*, vol. 10. Nashville: Abingdon Press, 2002.

CHAPTER SIX

Completing the Sermon Process

Difficult texts such as those considered in the last five chapters are not puzzles to be solved. The task of the preacher is not to take away the difficulty and show that the passages really are quite easy. They can be easy only in the sense that Jesus says his yoke is easy. Rather, the task of the preacher is to show precisely why the teaching is difficult, and to stress that the difficulty is an essential part of the biblical witness, a part of the gospel itself. In Hebrews 4:12 we read: "The word of God is living and active, sharper than any two-edged sword, piercing until it divides soul from spirit, joints from marrow." The preacher's task is to keep the sharpness and not let it be dulled. Furthermore, part of the task is to show that the teaching is hard not simply because of some personal failing or weakness on the part of individual church members, but because of the pressures and expectations of the culture in which we live. This can be a comforting word. In our individualistic culture, we tend to assume that all failings are simply personal, without giving much thought to the wider social context in which failure can become all too easy.

Assembling the Building Blocks

In preparing the sermon, it is first necessary to assemble certain building blocks. These are (1) the biblical passages and their interpretation, (2) understandings about our culture, and (3) awareness of any other elements that will affect the liturgical setting of the sermon. I will deal with these in order.

(1) The Biblical Passages

In each of the last five chapters we have looked at several biblical passages focusing on an issue that is difficult for Christians in our present culture to deal with. Surely we cannot include all of these passages in a single sermon, nor should we attempt to. The sermon needs to be based on a very specific text. At the same time, the discipline of studying all of these passages is essential as preparation for creating the sermon itself. A congregation needs to be assured that what the preacher is saying represents the heart of the biblical message and not simply a single passage taken out of context. This is even more important when it is a difficult or challenging text.

How can these passages be discovered? The preacher must be a student of Scripture, constantly discovering more and more interesting, unusual, and helpful passages. It is also useful to have a version of the Bible that has good cross-references.[1] This does not mean that one agrees that all of the cross-references are relevant, but it does give a place to begin. Such a reference Bible does not need to be the same translation as the one used for preaching. In fact, having a variety of translations is necessary in order to understand the nuances of the key words in the text. After a variety of texts have been selected to study, then commentaries are useful. They may also lead to further texts.

It is helpful for at least one of the biblical passages mentioned in the sermon to be fairly familiar to the congregation. In an age of biblical illiteracy this can be difficult. However, being able to bring in a phrase from the Lord's Prayer or the parable of the Prodigal Son—even at the end of the sermon, showing that it may mean something quite different from what we usually think—can reinforce the centrality of the message. It also makes the congregation look at the way our society may have softened the biblical message so that phrases like "our daily bread" have become watered down. It restores some sharpness to a familiar text.

It is necessary not only to look at texts that point in the same direction as the sermon, but also to deal with passages that point the opposite way. In the sermon that will be developed fully in this chapter, passages about God's love and forgiveness are contrasted with the difficult word about God's vengeance. This is done at the very beginning of the sermon precisely because such positive biblical words will be in the minds of many in the congregation, and could lead the congregation to dismiss whatever seems to contradict such sentiments.

(2) Understandings About Our Culture

The preacher must be clear about why the text is difficult. That is not always easy; it takes time and thought. It would be helpful to write out a list of reasons. The preacher needs to do a lot of soul-searching, for if the text is not difficult for the preacher, then it will be hard to deal with it in any way that will speak to the congregation. That is to say, if the preacher finds the verse quite easy not only to understand but also to live out, and yet assumes that the congregation will find it difficult, then the preacher may have trouble making a connection with the world in which the congregation lives. If the preacher really is part of the same culture as the congregation, then a careful self-examination will help the preacher understand why the text might be difficult, since the preacher also feels those difficulties. This approach also means the preacher is placing herself or himself in the midst of the congregation, listening to the text, and not apart from the congregation as the authority over it. The authority is the word of God in the biblical passage under which both the preacher and the congregation stand.

(3) Other Liturgical Elements

The preacher has the biblical studies and the list of reasons the message is difficult. That may be enough in preparation, but there are two other matters to be considered in addition to anything that is particular to that congregation or community. First, the liturgical season. If these sermons are a series in the Lenten season, then the overarching theme is the meaning of discipleship. If they occur just after Pentecost, then the theme may be the character and calling of the church, or the work of the Holy Spirit. Post-Easter sermons might stress the newness of life in the dawning kingdom. The season itself may give a clue as to how to begin or how to present the material.

The second additional concern is the sacraments. Is the sermon to be part of a worship service in which there is a baptism? If so, then the word about the difficult or countercultural character of the Christian life can be related to the meaning of baptism for all of us, and not only for the person being baptized. Even if there is no celebration of baptism during this particular service, the fact that the sermon is being preached to a baptized community can also be a starting point. Is there a communion service? Then the sermon needs to find a link between the message of the difficult life to which we are called, and the meaning of communion. It could be that communion reminds us of the covenant we have with God. It could be the sign of forgiveness for our past avoidance of the difficulty in discipleship. The Eucharist could stress the strength that we are given so we can follow the narrow way. The sacraments and the season together may suggest an approach to the text.

PUTTING IT ALL TOGETHER

Whatever the actual beginning, early in the sermon there needs to be a discussion of the particular cultural characteristic that will make the text difficult. This may be shown by means of an illustration or vignette, or it may simply be described. The starting point also could be the text itself, followed by a discussion of how strange it probably seems and why. The preacher might begin with something about the season, if that suggests clear connection with the text. However one begins, it is then necessary to bring in the other elements: the cultural issue and the biblical text. If a baptism occurred earlier in the service, that could be the starting point.

It is easier if both the beginning and the end are decided upon before the whole sermon is constructed. In other words, is there to be a tie-in with communion at the end? Is a familiar text to be at the end? Are there to be suggestions for the life of the congregation at the end?

This last item is very important. If the gospel really does contradict elements in our culture, then it is important that there be a supportive community—the church—that helps individual Christians and families keep on the difficult way of discipleship. That was part of the cause of the vitality of the early church. In our own day, however, often a sermon that points to what we should be leaves us feeling individually guilty, but with little sense of what to do except try harder. It is very helpful to stress that all of us find the way of discipleship difficult. It is not simply individual failings that have kept us from faithfulness, but powerful elements of the society in which we live that have blinded all of us to the meaning and demands of the gospel. If there are suggestions for how the congregation could shape its own life so that the members can find some support, that could make a powerful conclusion to a sermon and perhaps lead to further discussion within the congregation about the issue raised.

For instance, in relation to issues in the previous chapters, are there ways the life of the congregation could model what being satisfied with "enough" would look like? Are there ways in which a congregation could reverse in its life the tendency of our culture to separate single and married people? Are there ways in which a congregation could consciously look for some of its leadership among those who are not prominent in the wider society? Such suggestions give life to abstract ideas. They also make it clear that the preacher is not simply talking about how each member is challenged by the text, but even more how the congregation itself is challenged.

There can be no single formula for a sermon. However, having these building blocks at hand and then working with them in a creative and personal way makes presenting difficult texts significant and enriching in the life of a congregation. In the case of the difficult text used in chapter 2 concerning Paul's preference for celibacy, the following section could be the preacher's worksheet, showing the different building blocks. (It would probably be sketchier, since the preacher would have the issues more clearly in mind.)

1 Corinthians 7:1-8, 25-38

I. ON ONE HAND

1. Paul expected the end of history soon and therefore his advice is not for us, since we know he was wrong about how soon Christ would return.

2. It makes no sense in our culture to intend to remain single. Sex is a normal part of human life. Even in the church everything is family-oriented. The Protestant Reformation ended the thought

that celibacy was more pleasing to God than marriage. That is why we do not have to join monasteries.

3. The Old Testament is completely opposed to such an idea.

    (a) In Genesis 2:18, God said that it was "not good that the man should be alone." We are created to need the intimacy that such relationships provide.

    (b) The Song of Solomon shows the beauty of human love.

    (c) There is no emphasis at all on celibacy in the Old Testament. There was a duty to marry. We cannot assume such a total discrepancy between the Old Testament and Paul's views.

4. Other passages in the New Testament assume that marriage is preferable.

    (a) First Timothy 3:2-5 assumes that marriage and the successful managing of a family is required for bishops. First Timothy 3:8-12 requires the same for deacons.

    (b) First Timothy 5:14 gives preference for young widows to marry again and have children.

(If Paul wrote both 1 Corinthians and 1 Timothy, there is an even greater complication.)

II. ON THE OTHER HAND

1. In our own culture we no longer stress the need to "be fruitful and multiply." That was much of the Old Testament's basis for emphasizing marriage. Our problem is more overpopulation than the need for many children.

2. There are other passages in the New Testament that point to a different attitude toward family than what was in the Old Testament.

    (a) Luke 20:34-36: Jesus says that marriage is of this age, but those worthy of the new age do not marry.

    (b) Matthew 9:11-12: Jesus says that some have made themselves eunuchs for the sake of the kingdom.

    (c) Matthew 12:49: Jesus says those who do the Father's will are Jesus' brother and sister and mother.

3. In this passage in 1 Corinthians, Paul has two comments that need to be discussed:

(a) 7:26—"the impending crisis"—perhaps expected persecution.

(b) 7:29—"the appointed time has grown short"—not only the return of Christ, but the tribulation that may accompany that.

(c) Paul does not disagree with the Old Testament view for previous times in Israel's life. But for Christians things have changed; and that is the reason for a different view.

4. A brief portion of this text, 1 Corinthians 7:29-31, is used in the lectionary (Year B, Third Sunday After Epiphany or Ordinary Time). It is paired with Mark 1:14-20, the sons of Zebedee leaving their father and following Jesus

III. BASIC QUESTIONS

1. Paul may have been wrong about how soon Christ would return, but is he wrong that Christians do live in the new age—the new creation—in some very important ways? In other words, he may have been wrong about the end of the old age, but he was not wrong about the beginning of the new age. We live in both. To what degree does the passage have to do with the new age in which we live, and not merely the end of the old one that has not come?

2. Has the church so settled down in this world that it has lost any sense that we as Christians are to live at least to some degree in the new creation?

3. Protestants during the Reformation period ended monasticism but since then have found it difficult to fully incorporate singles into the congregation. Singles may be in separate groups being ministered to, but are they fully part of a congregation in which families are the norm?

ANOTHER EXAMPLE

From the difficult texts used in the previous chapters, this one from chapter 5 concerning God's vengeance has been selected to provide another sermon example. Here is the worksheet for this sermon:

Romans 12:14–13:4

I. WHY IT IS A DIFFICULT PASSAGE FOR US

1. We cannot think of God as vengeful. God is forgiving and loving, not vengeful.

2. If we do not try to overcome evil by attacking it, it will only get worse.

3. Is God involved in human violence?

4. Isn't "heaping burning coals" just another way of getting revenge?

5. Aren't there some enemies it is humanly impossible to love?

6. Parts of this text are so familiar we often really do not hear how radical it is.

7. What does it mean to "leave room for the wrath of God"?

II. OTHER PASSAGES

1. Matthew 5:44—love your enemies

2. Luke 6:27-28—bless those who curse you

3. James 3:9-10—out of the same mouth come blessing and cursing

4. Isaiah 10:5-7, 12—"Assyria, the rod of my wrath"

5. Genesis 4:8-15—the mark God put on Cain

6. Psalm 137:7-9—happy are those who take vengeance on our enemies

7. Deuteronomy 32:34-43—"Vengeance is mine,…I kill and I make alive."

8. Proverbs 25:21-22—heaping burning coals

9. Romans 13:1-4—referring to civil government

III. OTHER BUILDING BLOCKS

1. Particular word studies: *vengeance*

2. Does it appear in the lectionary? Where? What other lessons are used with it?

3. Church history: Marcion

IV. BASIC QUESTIONS

1. Why does Paul think God's vengeance is a help for loving our enemies?

2. How can we relate Paul's understanding to our own enemies?

The worksheet above was developed before the sermon was written. The following is the sermon that was actually preached. In the service the Old Testament lesson was Genesis 4:8-15, which is mentioned in the outline above. The passage from Romans 12 is read at the end of the sermon as well as at the beginning, with the hope that after the sermon it might speak to the hearer in a new way.

The Text: Romans 12:14-21

Bless those who persecute you; bless and do not curse them. Rejoice with those who rejoice, weep with those who weep. Live in harmony with one another; do not be haughty, but associate with the lowly; do not claim to be wiser than you are. Do not repay anyone evil for evil, but take thought for what is noble in the sight of all. If it is possible, so far as it depends on you, live peaceably with all. Beloved, never avenge yourselves, but leave room for the wrath of God; for it is written, "Vengeance is mine, I will repay, says the Lord." No, "if your enemies are hungry, feed them; if they are thirsty, give them something to drink; for by doing this you will heap burning coals on their heads." Do not be overcome by evil, but overcome evil with good.

A STRANGE VIEW OF GOD

This passage from Paul's Letter to the Romans is both familiar and strange. We are used to some of its major themes: love your enemies, turn the other cheek, bless those who persecute you. These are familiar commands, even if they are among the most difficult characteristics of the Christian life. What is strange and unfamiliar is Paul's rationale for such behavior. If I were to assume Paul's rationale without reading the rest of the passage, I would expect him to say that we are to imitate God—God who loves sinners just as the father loved the prodigal son; God who loved us even while we were sinners; God who sends rain on the just and the unjust. We are to be forgiving as God forgives, and merciful as God is merciful, and loving as God is loving. All of that would be familiar and the way Paul and the rest of Scripture often admonish us. But that is not what Paul does. What he says here is that we are not to seek vengeance against enemies, not because we need to imitate God in this matter, but rather because vengeance belongs to God and in this matter we are not to imitate God.

It is difficult for us to think of God as vengeful—seeking vengeance. Paul here is quoting an Old Testament passage, and perhaps we think that such sentiments belong there but not in the New Testament. Yet Paul quotes this with approval. It fits what he wishes to say. We are not to seek vengeance because vengeance is God's prerogative, not ours. In fact, Paul says that we are not to seek vengeance because we need "to leave room for the wrath of God." It is as though evil actions leave a space for vengeance. Justice calls for something to be done. Either we can preempt God and fill that space with our own anger and retribution or we can leave the space for God to fill. "Beloved, never avenge yourselves, but leave room for the wrath of God; for it is written, 'Vengeance is mine, I will repay, says the Lord.' " The quotation comes from the Song of Moses in Deuteronomy, when God admonishes Israel for trusting in its own strength and in foreign gods for its defense (Deuteronomy 32:34-36). Only God can truly defend them. Only God can bring them real vindication.

Vengeance: it is a terrible word. It has overtones of hatred, of a drive to get even with those who have wronged us. It is not surprising, then, that we have difficulty with passages in the Bible that speak of our God as a God of vengeance. The root of our word *vengeance* in English picks up the nuances of both the Hebrew and the Greek terms it is used to translate. Both *vengeance* and *vindication* come from the same Latin root. An avenger is one who brings revenge, yes, but also one who brings vindication. For us *vindication* is a positive word. It implies being shown to be innocent or being defended against enemies who would defame or defeat us. Vindication is good, but being vindictive is the same as being vengeful. We rarely use the term *avenger* because it seems violent, and yet the word *vindicator* really means the same thing and is quite acceptable. So the word *vengeance* must be understood as both punishment on evildoers and bringing justice to the wrongfully treated. In God's hands, vengeance seeks to accomplish justice, vindicating the oppressed and judging the oppressor. Such action is not a denial of God's love but rather a means for demonstrating it. God even loves and vindicates those against whom God has previously exercised vengeance for their evil actions.

In our hands, however, it is a different matter. If we seek to vindicate ourselves or others, then God cannot be the vindicator. God is far better at the task of being a vindicator than we are.

God can be both loving and avenging. We cannot be. It is no accident that the same Song of Moses that speaks of vengeance as belonging to God alone also has God saying these words:

> See now that I, even I, am he;
>   there is no god besides me.
> I kill and I make alive;
>   I wound and I heal. (Deuteronomy 32:39)

We cannot do that. We can kill, but we cannot make alive; nor can we be sure of healing when we wound. God can use Assyria as the rod of his wrath against Israel and then judge Assyria. We have no such ability. Vengeance is safe with God, for no mistakes will be made, and God has the power of life and death. With us, however, it is a different matter. Our anger can lash out at those we discover later are innocent. Our vindictiveness can permanently harm relationships and bring no healing and no restoration. In the Sermon on the Mount we are warned not to judge lest we be judged with the same sort of vindictive judgment (Matthew 7:1-2).

Think again of that strange passage from Genesis that was read earlier. Cain clearly was guilty of murder. He knew it, and God knew it. God has punished him by making him a fugitive. But Cain fears for his life, afraid that those who find him will kill him. God's words are very interesting; no one is to touch Cain. And God puts a mark on him not as a sign of Cain's guilt, but as the sign of God's protection. God says: "Whoever kills Cain will suffer a sevenfold vengeance." God is protecting the guilty from the vengeance of others. God is taking care of the matter, and we are not to intervene. This is exactly what Paul means by "leaving room for the wrath of God."

Paul does not mean that only in the life to come will evildoers be punished. In the next chapter of Romans, chapter 13, Paul points to civil governments that seek to maintain justice. He writes: "[The governing] authority does not bear the sword in vain! It is the servant of God to execute wrath on the wrongdoer" (v. 4). Chapter divisions in the Bible are frequently more of a hindrance than a help. We so often read Paul's words about civil governments in chapter 13 as though they were a new topic. But they are not. Paul continues here the explanation that evildoers will be taken care of by God and not by private vendettas or personal retribution. Sometimes it is the state that does this; sometimes God employs other means.

The question at hand, however, is why does Paul use the reasoning he does for loving our enemies? What does God's vengeance have to do with it? The passage we read begins with the words: "Bless those who persecute you; bless and do not curse them." The words mean more than "do not be angry." They mean that not only are we not to wish our enemies ill, we are to pray that they will prosper, that good things will happen to them. This does not mean praying only that God will show them the error of their ways. Obviously, if we are wishing them well, it would be hard to plan vengeance against them. We are to love our enemies and pray that God will bless them. We can do this with confidence because God is our vindicator, and God will work out justice in the matter.

What Paul and Matthew and other New Testament writers understand is that we cannot be loving sometimes and hateful other times. We must be single-minded. What Matthew says is that a good tree bears good fruit—and it is by our fruit we will be known. Our fruit is to be love. To the degree that we are not totally loving we are not yet a totally good tree. We still have work to do. What James writes is this:

> From the same mouth come blessing and cursing. My brothers and sisters, this ought not to be so. Does a spring pour forth from the same opening both fresh and brackish water? Can a fig tree, my brothers and sisters, yield olives, or a grapevine figs? No more can salt water yield fresh. (James 3:10-12)

To acknowledge that vengeance belongs to God and not to us allows us to concentrate single-mindedly on becoming loving people. At the same time, it makes clear that justice does need to be done, and in God's hands it will be. In fact, it would be difficult to imagine being able to love our enemies if we did not believe that vindication for the innocent would occur—and that we do not have to stop our loving for it to happen.

To love our enemies, to show it by truly blessing those who persecute us, this is probably the most difficult task of the Christian life. How much easier it is to have "righteous indignation" against those who attack us—and, on the basis of our righteous indignation, seek to balance the scales of justice by attacking them. It is the natural reaction, and yet, in Paul's words, such actions mean that we have been overcome by evil rather than having overcome evil by good. We so easily step into the breach and do not "leave room for the wrath of God." We can justify our actions on all sorts of grounds; but for Paul the bottom line then remains that we have been overcome by the same evil we have sought to destroy.

Does this mean we should just let injustice happen and not care about it? No, it does not. We may seek to involve the civil government on behalf of the victim. As citizens of a democracy, unlike the Roman Empire of Paul's day, we may use our role as citizens to seek laws to protect the innocent or to insist that laws be followed. That will not prevent opposition and even martyrdom. But our task is just like Paul's and the Roman Christians' in the first century: we must love our enemies and bless those who persecute and oppress.

It sounds impossible; and, humanly speaking, it is. Probably none of us has reached that point yet. What this passage tells us is what to do when we find ourselves seeking vengeance or even wishing for it. First, we are to remember that vengeance is not our task, but God's. Second, we are to remember that we have now identified a person or group for whom we are to pray that God will bless. Our task is to change ourselves so that we may be more open and useful for God's purposes.

We live in a time of great conflict and division. In so many parts of the world, vengeance seems to be a way of life between ethnic groups; and the cycle of violence goes back decades, if not centuries. Yet conflict is not only in the world at large but also within our churches. What would happen if within the church we practiced these words of Paul? If we prayed for good things to happen to those in our denomination who disagree with us on the divisive issues of the day? What if both sides really did believe that God is the one who will judge and vindicate, and that meanwhile we are to bless each other and use the occasion to grow in love?

Finally, in this passage Paul quotes not only from Deuteronomy but also from the book of Proverbs: "If your enemies are hungry, feed them; if they are thirsty, give them something to drink; for by doing this you will heap burning coals on their heads" (Romans 12:20). To me, this always sounded as though by being nice you were trying to get revenge in a roundabout way—after all, a heap of burning coals on one's head is hardly pleasant. But in the context here Paul cannot mean that. Rather, the hope is that by responding with good rather than evil, the heart of the enemy may at least be brought to a sense of remorse. The concluding verse of the chapter makes it clear: "Do not be overcome by evil, but overcome evil with good." If we respond as a friend to one who is our enemy, it is clear their evil has not conquered us.

Paul does not make loving our enemies any easier, but his rationale of trusting God as the vindicator rather than ourselves shows us a perspective that helps in that task. Hear again the words of the lesson:

> Bless those who persecute you; bless and do not curse them. Rejoice with those who rejoice, weep with those who weep. Live in harmony with one another; do not be haughty, but associate with the lowly; do not claim to be wiser than you are. Do not repay anyone evil for evil, but take thought for what is noble in the sight of all. If it is possible, so far as it depends on you, live peaceably with all. Beloved, never avenge yourselves, but leave room for the wrath of God; for it is written, "Vengeance is mine, I will repay, says the Lord." No, "if your enemies are hungry, feed them; if they are thirsty, give them something to drink; for by doing this you will heap burning coals on their heads." Do not be overcome by evil, but overcome evil with good.

(This is the end of the sermon. In many settings a prayer would be appropriate at this point.)

Some Final Words

The somewhat scholastic approach used above—raising objections and support from the Bible, common sense, and so forth—means the preacher begins by listening to the text in the same way the congregation will. The preacher has become part of the congregation at the beginning of the preparation, even though the preacher will probably move from that stance later in the sermon. The preacher needs to create the list of objections or questions before checking with commentaries, listening to the text not as an academic but as a faithful Christian. This approach gives the congregation permission to raise questions or to recognize that their questions are acceptable. Often laypeople think that it is improper to question a biblical text, to say that it makes no sense, or that it contradicts what they have always believed the Christian faith was about. If the preacher publicly voices these questions, it helps the congregation approach Scripture authentically. Once such a list has been created, then commentaries, lexicons, and all the rest will be helpful, and the preacher can become the resident scholar. The expertise, however, will be directed at the issues with which the congregation can identify. Though many biblical passages have been studied in preparation for preaching, it is still clear that there is a specific biblical passage with which the sermon is concerned. The other passages looked at are for support and clarification.

No "method" of preaching can guarantee that a difficult passage will be heard and understood, or that a congregation will change its ways because of the sermon. It is the Holy Spirit and not the preacher that makes possible the true hearing of God's word with conviction. However, in the whole service of worship in which the sermon is a part, there are ways the congregation can be helped to be more open to hearing difficult texts.

Notes

1. Can the Consumer Ever Be Satisfied?

1. Barclay M. Newman and Philip C. Stine, *A Translator's Handbook on the Gospel of Matthew* (New York: United Bible Societies, 1988), 75-76, 198.

2. Ambrose, "On the Duties of the Clergy," bk. 1, ch. 28, sect. 132, in *A Select Library of Nicene and Post-Nicene Fathers of the Christian Church* (Grand Rapids: Wm. B. Eerdmans Publishing Co., 1955), 23.

3. W. Sibley Towner, "Ecclesiastes," in vol. 5 of *The New Interpreter's Bible* (Nashville: Abingdon Press, 1997), 311-19, 343.

4. Raymond C. Van Leeuwen, "The Book of Proverbs," in vol. 5 of *The New Interpreter's Bible* (Nashville: Abingdon Press, 1997), 253.

2. Celibacy? You're Kidding!

1. Will Deming, *Paul on Marriage and Celibacy: The Hellenistic Background of 1 Corinthians 7* (Cambridge: Cambridge University Press, 1995), 52, 60-61, 95.

2. J. Paul Sampley, "The First Letter of Paul to the Corinthians," in vol. 10 of *The New Interpreter's Bible* (Nashville: Abingdon Press, 2002), 869.

3. Ibid., 872.

4. Paul VI, "Encyclical Letter on Priestly Celibacy," 24 June 1967, sect. 10, in vol. 2 of *Vatican II: More Post-Conciliar Documents,* edited by Austin Flannery (Northport, New York: Costello Publishing Company, 1982), 287.

5. See John Calvin, *Institutes of the Christian Religion,* 4.8.3.

6. Phyllis McGinley, *Saint-Watching* (New York: The Viking Press, 1969), 216.

7. R. Pierce Beaver, *All Loves Excelling* (Grand Rapids: Wm. B. Eerdmans Publishing Company, 1968), 179-80.

3. Blest Handkerchiefs and Demons

1. There is a very interesting book written by a Roman Catholic priest/theologian who was a missionary in Africa for many years. It is helpful in seeing how a

nonscientific culture views the world and the biblical message. Aylward Shorter, *Jesus and the Witchdoctor* (Maryknoll, N.Y.: Orbis Books, 1980).

2. Ralph P. Martin, *Ephesians, Colossians, and Philemon,* Interpretation: A Bible Commentary for Teaching and Preaching (Atlanta: John Knox, 1991), 127-29.

3. See Justo L. González, *The Gospel of the Spirit* (Maryknoll, N.Y.: Orbis Books, 2001), 221-24.

4. Robert W. Wall, "The Acts of the Apostles," in vol. 10 of *The New Interpreter's Bible* (Nashville: Abingdon Press, 2002), 269.

5. Ibid., 267.

4. Shouldn't We Try to Get Ahead?

1. Efren J. M. Montalva, *La herencia teresiana* (Madrid: Editorial de Espiritualidad, 1975), 190.

2. See, for example, John Calvin, *Institutes of the Christian Religion,* 2.20.44; B. A. Garrish, *Grace and Gratitude: The Eucharistic Theology of John Calvin* (Minneapolis: Fortress Press, 1992), 87-88; Catechism of the Church of Geneva, particularly the first seven questions.

3. John Calvin, "Reply to Sadolet," in *Calvin: Theological Treatises,* vol. 22 of The Library of Christian Classics (Philadelphia: The Westminster Press, 1954), 228.

4. James D. Martin, *The Book of Judges* (London: Cambridge University Press, 1975), 35.

5. M. Eugene Boring, "Matthew," in vol. 8 of *The New Interpreter's Bible* (Nashville: Abingdon Press, 1995), 392-94.

6. Ibid., 398.

7. Douglas R. A. Hare, *Matthew,* Interpretation: A Bible Commentary for Teaching and Preaching (Louisville: John Knox Press, 1993), 234.

8. Donald Senior, *Matthew,* Abingdon New Testament Commentaries (Nashville: Abingdon Press, 1998), 225.

5. The God of Vengeance

1. N. T. Wright, "The Letter to the Romans," in vol. 10 of *The New Interpreter's Bible* (Nashville: Abingdon Press, 2002), 714.

2. Ambrose, *Cain and Abel*, bk. 2, ch. 9, sect. 38, *The Fathers of the Church,* vol. 42, translated by John J. Savage (New York: Fathers of the Church, 1961), 437.

3. C. E. B. Cranfield, *Commentary on Romans 12–13,* Scottish Journal of Theology Occasional Paper No.12 (Edinburgh: Oliver and Boyd, 1965), 56-57.

4. Wright, "Letter to the Romans."

5. Cranfield, *Commentary on Romans,* 52.

6. Completing the Sermon Process

1. See, for example, *New American Standard Bible* ®, © Copyright 1960, 1962, 1963, 1968, 1971, 1972, 1973, 1975, 1977, 1995 by The Lockman Foundation (www.Lockman.org).